HALF OF THE WORLD IN LIGHT

CAMINO DEL SOL

A Latina and Latino Literary Series

HALF OF THE WORLD IN LIGHT

| *New and Selected Poems* |

JUAN FELIPE HERRERA

With a Foreword by
FRANCISCO A. LOMELÍ

THE UNIVERSITY OF ARIZONA PRESS | TUCSON

The University of Arizona Press
© 2008 Juan Felipe Herrera
All rights reserved

Library of Congress Cataloging-in-Publication Data

Herrera, Juan Felipe.
    Half of the world in light : new and selected poems /
Juan Felipe Herrera ; with a foreword by Francisco A.
Lomelí.
        p. cm.
    ISBN 978-0-8165-2703-8 (pbk. : alk. paper) I. Title.
PS3558.E74H36   2008
811'.54—dc22   2007044782

Publication of this book is made possible in part by
the proceeds of a permanent endowment created with
the assistance of a Challenge Grant from the National
Endowment for the Humanities, a federal agency.

Manufactured in the United States of America on acid-free,
archival-quality paper containing a minimum of 30% post-
consumer waste and processed chlorine free.

13 12 11 10 09   6 5 4 3 2

For Margarita, the one—with the flowers
For Rosa Quintana, RIP

For Connie Hales
For Lauro Flores
For Al Arteaga
For Renato Rosaldo, Jr.
For Sasha Quintana
For Bella Mansour
For Marvin Bell
For Li-Young Lee
For Gerald Stern
For Bernice Zamora
For Matt Lippman
For Manuel Martin-Rodriguez
For Francisco X. Alarcón
For Phil Levine
For Mauricio Kilwein-Guevara
For Rubén Martinez
For Francisco Lomelí & María Herrera-Sobek
For Rigoberto Gonzalez
For John Martínez
For Lorna Dee Cervantes
For Ernie Paz
For my great-grandmother, Vicentita Palomares

For Patti Hartmann
Para el Maestro, Don Luis Leal—

Verde que te quiero verde
—FEDERICO GARCÍA LORCA, "Romance Sonámbulo"

CONTENTS

FOREWORD | JUAN FELIPE HERRERA

Trajectory and Metamorphosis of a Chicano Poet Laureate

FRANCISCO A. LOMELÍ

Chicano writings since the 1960s have spiraled and evolved into a fully legitimate body of literary expression that has transcended its own making. There are numerous landmark moments in its creativity that have left indelible imprints, such as Rodolfo "Corky" Gonzales's epic poem *Yo soy Joaquín* (1967), Luis Valdez's revolutionary *Actos* (1971), Alurista's tour de force collection *Floricanto en Aztlán* (1971), Rudolfo Anaya's foundational text *Bless Me, Ultima* (1972), Sandra Cisneros's moving *The House on Mango Street* (1984), Ana Castillo's groundbreaking *The Mixquiahuala Letters* (1985), Gloria Anzaldúa's profound *Borderlands/La Frontera: The New Mestiza* (1987), Josefina López's provocative *Real Women Have Curves* (1992), and others. However, no one has encompassed more literary space of substance, renovation, and originality than Juan Felipe Herrera, who stands out as perhaps the most innovative alchemist of metaphoric language and a voice of the overall Chicano experience. It is not exaggerated to state that he embodies a one-person vanguard in constant movement, metamorphosing into new forms and styles by challenging convention while blazing new paths of expression. He is both daring and artful par excellence; he does not limit himself to deconstruction or subversion because, above all, he proposes mindful imagery while creating new imaginary constructs. As a visionary kaleidoscope, he reconfigures images and ideas into Picasso-like confabulations in order to better see the edges of human existence and appreciate the core. His writings reveal masterful word configurations and connotations by splicing and mixing not unlike those in the style of ee cummings, Dadaism, Francisco de Quevedo, Brazilian poetic calligraphy, and Chicano poets Alurista, José Antonio Burciaga, Ricardo Sánchez, and Gloria Anzaldúa. A true Renaissance individual, Juan Felipe Herrera is the inimitable synthesizer, a factory of hybridity, and a maelstrom of nonconforming productiveness. A rare talent with a restless poetics, he is the consummate poet among poets who has developed through time and survived—through his many contributions—the many twists of change. In fact, he has probably evolved more than any other Chicano poet, having gone through a variety of stages and transformations, always reinventing himself into a more mature and seasoned voice.

A prodigious presence in the field of Chicano literature since his early beginnings in the late 1960s, he has also contributed decisively to theater as an actor, to music as a singer and musician, to festivals and gatherings of performance poetry as an organizer, to multimedia and performance ensembles as a founder, to photography as an ardent collector of family and community archives, to mural and visual art as the director of the Centro Cultural de la Raza in San Diego and other cultural venues, and to films as a scriptwriter. His eclectic range of intellectual and community activity is well chronicled as legendary in San Diego, the San Francisco Bay Area, Fresno, and Riverside. With some twenty-four books to date, he has become the leading poetic voice in Chicano circles, while cognizant that his writings go beyond a single genre, label, or style. His overall *oeuvre* is characterized by carefully crafted works of experimentation and inventiveness, almost always marking a *happening*, albeit at first demonstrating a slow production up to 1984. Since then, however, he has produced a steady stream of groundbreaking, award-winning, landmark works, such as *Exiles of Desire* (1983), *Mayan Drifter: Chicano Poet in the Lowlands of America* (1997), *Border-Crosser with a Lamborghini Dream* (1999), *Lotería Cards and Fortune Poems: A Book of Lives* (with linocuts by Artemio Rodríguez, 1999), *CrashBoomLove: A Novel in Verse* (1999), *Notebooks of a Chile Verde Smuggler* (2002), *Cinnamon Girl: Letters Found Inside a Cereal Box* (2005), and more. He currently stands out as the recipient of the most awards in Chicano literary circles, including twice the Chicano Literary Prize from the University of California at Irvine, the El Paso Chicano Poetry Prize from the University of Texas, twice the

Americas Award, the Hungry Mind Award of Distinction, twice the Latino Literary Hall of Fame, and an Independent Publishers Award. In addition, his contributions to children's and young adult literature have garnered him considerable attention thanks to numerous national awards, for example, the Smithsonian Notable Children's Book for *Calling the Doves* (1995), the Smithsonian Notable Book of the Year for *The Upside Down Boy* (2000), America's Award for Children and Young Adult Literature for *Cinnamon Girl: Letters Found Inside a Cereal Box* (2005), and the Tomás Rivera Mexican American Children's Book Award for *Downtown Boy* (2007).

Juan Felipe Herrera has indeed come a long way: from youthful reflections on the unfolding of history in the late 1960s to mature meditations on the complexities of such contemporary regions of social tension as the Middle East in the twenty-first century. Only a wide lens of experience can appropriate such spaces so poetically as to render them meaningful. In that regard, he has become a major voice in the international poetry scene, as evinced by the sheer number of works anthologized and invitations to public forums. His initial incursion into poetry was greatly influenced by the wanderings[1] of his migrant farmworker family and unstable social settings. He at first sought a place into which he could fit. Fortuitously, in San Diego in his teens, he met Alurista,[2] who later became the leading voice of the Chicano Movement poetry. The two created a unique bond of youthful bohemianism that seemed to spawn a new trend in incantatory poetry, reclaiming their cultural roots and, in the process, contributing to the creation of Chicano cultural nationalism. The two formed an enviable duo of creativity and determination, with Alurista taking the initial risk by publishing his noteworthy work *Floricanto en Aztlán* (1971), which revolutionized literary expression through its bilingual/Spanglish modality, while underscoring the regenerative role of Aztlán as the mythological homeland for Chicanos. Alurista's direct influence is apparent in Herrera's first work, *Rebozos of Love/We Have Woven/Sudor de Pueblos/On Our Back* (1974), but he also manages to exhibit his own signature and prowess through an Oriental sense of yin and yang between text and image, form and content, and Spanish and English. By revering languages as codices of meaning, Herrera displays his linguistic dexterity by creating a philosophical playfulness through rapid-fire imagery and neologisms:

cuerpos of man de luz	(bodies of man of light)
and woman to earth rise	and woman to earth rise
songrise	songrise
razarise	peoplerise
que sí	definitely
desnudos	naked
sin nudos	without knots
sembrando	sowing
besando	kissing
u	a
n	h
c	e
o	a
r	r
a	t
z	
ó	
n[3]	

The free-flowing verses suggest continuity instead of linear constructions, thus providing one long poem of constant intervals that change in shape, typed text versus handwriting, and even writing juxtaposed with or accompanied by visual illustrations. As Santiago Vaquera-Vásquez writes, "The poems are also presented as 'chants,' linking them into an oral poetic tradition. These poem-chants are performances aimed at connecting with a larger indigenous shared collective. There is a sense of creation and intent toward a unification of Chicano identity."[4] The impulse is not only culturally nationalist in scope but also spiritualist and cosmological in content. Herrera's many references to a new beginning allude to the Chicano Renaissance[5] in an effort to reestablish harmony through the sacred act of blossoming. As the two critics of *Chicano Perspectives in Literature: A Critical and Annotated Bibliography* (Lomelí and Urioste 1976) point out, a definite mysticism emerges that hints at a "cosmic whole by uniting dualities: *señor-señora*, wind and rain, love and energy, time-space."[6] Herrera, therefore, produces via poetry a vision of a reachable utopia in order to intimate a new social order as long as the Amerindian (indigenous) values are honored and cultivated. Much like John Lennon's song "Imagine" from 1971, Herrera's poetry conjures up possibilities and potential in a fair new world in order to imagine beyond the box.

Notwithstanding, in many ways his inspirations are Latin American through the fusion of multiple styles and influences, although as a bilingual and bicultural Chicano he remains open and receptive to any influence that might feed his curiosity and protean worldview. He might not be the Modernist Rubén Darío of Chicano poetry, defining and setting the parameters for Chicano aesthetics, yet he could be called the Vanguard Pablo Neruda of a socially committed sentiment and verve, whose intuitive approach defies classification. Or, he might be best situated between two other giants: Vicente Huidobro, whose *Creacionismo* underscored art for art's sake in seeking the metaphor as the lifeblood of language, and, perhaps even more so, César Vallejo, whose democratic but seditious pessimism mirrored the angst of his era. Moreover, Herrera is "alluvial" in that he embraces residual gazes from the anarchistic Beat Generation that were later fueled and reinforced by the innocent philosophy of the Hippie Generation, and of course that led into the tantalizing cultural politics of identity within the messianic Chicano Movement. In short, he does not represent only one literary movement but a rainbow of many tendencies: cultural nationalism, skeptical politics, an anti-conventional literary posture (in particular, the anti-novel as seen in *Cinnamon Girl: Letters Found Inside a Cereal Box*), hardcore barrio sensibilities, modern allegories, postmodern impulses, transborder postulates, post–Chicano Movement discourses, analyses of rituals, and newer explorations into experimental calligraphy and the aesthetics of chaos. In his writings we find depth, dimension, and desire coming together thanks to ambiguity or paradox, like Quetzalcóatl (the plumed serpent), the Sphinx, and a satyr. In a review in 1989,[7] Marvin Bell captures key elements of Herrera's modus operandi:

> Juan Felipe is a storyteller, a surrealist, and polemicist all at once, and
> as a writer he goes beyond the sometimes brittle and insular thought
> model we are taught to recognize as poetry into an array of forms
> for play and politics. By it sinuosity and vibrancy, and by its octopus

reach into sources, such poetry makes the argument between poetic formalists and informalists appear to be taking place in a closet.

Originally from humble beginnings, Herrera has lived on the edge and in the forefront of new literary developments. His twenty-four books of poetry, novels in verse, narratives mixed with memoir, testimonials combined with journalistic treatises, and transgeneric narrations[8] clearly show a writer of multiple inspirations, ranging from the highly philosophical to the *rasquache*[9] political, from the irreverent to the socially engaged, or from the subliminal lyricist to the stubbornly quixotic. Essentially a fertile rhapsodist of passion and conviction, his works tend to be exercises into experimentation in form and nuance, that is, into stretching imagery and concepts, or minimalist minutiae, into free-flowing fragments that gain coherence through the magic of his poetry. His reputation for flair in the unexpected has enhanced his standing in literary circles, as reinforced by an uncanny versatility, notably his ability to speak in various tongues: from the monologues of indigeneity to the iconic metaphors of Allen Ginsberg, from Mark Twain picaresque to Cantinflas humor, from Jack Kerouac overtones to César Chávez spiritualism, from border Spanglish to street-smart punk, from a layperson's folklore to highfalutin philosophy, from the underside of marginalization to the excess of affluence, from the farmworker fields to the battleground in Israel, from the rhythms of jazz to the seductive lyrics of hip-hop and punk rock, from the concrete to the metaphysical, from melodious cadences to visual flashes, from a performer's pathos to Octavio Paz's poetic theory of re-experiencing the instant, and from a pious but rebellious iconoclast to a Chicano warrior *bato* with multiple identities as well as tonalities. His virtuosity is undeniable, his talent universally acclaimed, and his eclecticism unmatched. As Lauro H. Flores succinctly notes, "Juan Felipe Herrera is one of the finest, most innovative, and most challenging contemporary Chicano poets."[10]

Since the beginning of his most productive period in 1985 with *Exiles of Desire*, Herrera has risen in stature while expanding his repertoire in terms of subject and thematics. His persona before this period had a distinctive omnipresence in the various literary circles in which he moved, but thereafter his persona and his work truly blended into one looming in greatness. For example, his surprising portrayal of barrio dwellers in *Exiles of Desire* is moving, raw, and revealing, approaching a mythology of their struggle in a harsh environment:

> . . . Only tall faceless figures
> of pain flutter across the bridge. They pace in charred suits,
> the hands lift, point and ache and fly at sunset as cold dark
> birds. . . .[11]

Akrílica (1989), a title that echoes the inventiveness of Vicente Huidobro's penchant for neologisms, brings together a large collection of Spanish/English poems in the form of sketches from the 1980s, demonstrating a more mature and confident writer whose poetic indulgence appears limitless. His cleverness in format corresponds well with his assertive examination into topics he considers important. The variety and depth of the many expressionistic sketches range from prosaic divagations to a string of haikus, from dramatic scenes to a diary entry. Herrera combines techniques of visual art with verses and testimonies to provide a highly contemplative potential of what social poetry can uncover.

Herrera has also produced a collection of works that tend to combine serious treatments of social phenomena with humor and wit, thus universalizing feelings and circumstances. His books *Border-Crosser with a Lamborghini Dream* (1999), *Lotería Cards and Fortune Poems: A Book of Lives* (1999), *CrashBoomLove: A Novel in Verse* (1999), *Giraffe on Fire* (2001), and *Notebooks of a Chile Verde Smuggler* (2002) represent a prolific flurry within a short time of his innate creativity blended with social concerns, paradoxes, and contradictions. His knack for surprising the reader with untold images raises the ante of his productivity. For example, in *Border-Crosser*, he writes:

Calling all tomato pickers, the ones wearing death frowns instead of jackets
Calling all orange & lemon carriers, come down the ladder to this hole
Calling all chile pepper sack humpers, you, yes, you the ones with a crucifix[12]

With the other books of this period Herrera proves that he is able to tap into a rich wealth of material that continues to germinate new poetry. *Lotería Cards and Fortune Poems*, for instance, offers an original collaboration between Herrera the poet and Artemio Rodríguez, an artist from Mexico, to create an extremely innovative work by rewriting the style and content of Mexican lottery figures (a kind of bingo), adding to their cultural relevance and tradition. In this game of chance, playfulness becomes the central objective while cultural tidbits of meaning are pondered. The result is a milestone in Chicano creativity for the dialogue the poet establishes with tradition. Herrera's creative zaniness (e.g., "Juantoomany" and "La Llorona's last tear") explores family in a well-veiled testimonial incursion into various pasts to better understand the dialectics between world, regional, and biographical history. In *CrashBoomLove*, he produces a Chicano novel in verse after Ana Castillo's *The Mixquiahuala Letters* (1986), nonetheless a novelty for his spirited and audacious capacity for blending young adult dilemmas with adult thematics.

Among his most recent productions, *Cinnamon Girl: Letters Found Inside a Cereal Box*, his second novel in verse, stands out for its ability to bridge young adult literature with sophisticated writing consisting of unpredictable poetry/ prose and unbridled creativity. The result is a complex work of imagined biography combined with memory and hope. The seductive experimentation with language and secrecy opens up possibilities for intra-historical accounts of personal search against the backdrop of 9/11. Herrera has consequently shattered boundaries while plunging his shovel into the ground of new topics where the ethnic experience is as American as 9/11.

Although Herrera currently holds the important Tomás Rivera Endowed Chair in Chicano literature at the University of California at Riverside, his place in American literary circles has expanded considerably beyond the Chicano canon. He moves freely and defiantly against ghettoized notions of literature and away from popular consumerist literary expression. He stands out as a poetic phenomenon for his robust productivity. But most of all he is a uniquely American writer whose ethnicity conditions his *ars poetica* without constraining it. In this way, he provides new perspectives and vistas into the American mind and psyche as well as into a globalized or transnational sense of self.

NOTES

1. Santiago Vaquera-Vásquez, in his article "Juan Felipe Herrera (1948–)," mentions a "wandering poetics" as the central motif of his sensibility and formation, comparable to a tabula rasa of his ever-evolving writings (see Vaquera-Vásquez, 281–98).

2. The encounter is described in some detail by Sesshu Foster in "From Logan to the Mission" (68–87).

3. See *Rebozos of Love/We Have Woven/Sudor de Pueblos/On Our Back* (52).

4. Vaquera-Vásquez, p. 283.

5. This concept was first proposed by Philip D. Ortego in his seminal article from 1971 titled "The Chicano Renaissance," subsequently expanded by Juan Rodríguez in "El florecimiento de la literatura chicana."

6. See the same work by Francisco A. Lomelí and Donaldo W. Urioste, p. 26.

7. Bell, "A Poet's Sampler," p. 6.

8. Such a concept occurs when genres are combined or blended into a new admixture quite different from its original singular form. Ana Castillo, in a presentation at the University of California, Santa Barbara, on May 23, 2006, referred to this as "genre jumping," which applies equally to Juan Felipe Herrera.

9. *Rasquache*, or funky aesthetics, partly inspired by what is traditionally considered "low-class" or "riff-raff" art, has been best described and studied by Tomás Ybarra-Frausto in "Rasquachismo: A Chicano Sensibility." He claims that such art actually possesses a fundamentally subversive orientation by mocking "highbrow art" and consequently juxtaposing it critically to what art does by altering the original perceptions. Other art critics, such as Amalia Mesa-Bains, have also added to the concept. Alicia Gaspar de Alba (10–14, 25, 243) is another critic to focus on the complex issue.

10. Flores, "Juan Felipe Herrera (1948–)," p. 137.

11. Herrera, *Exiles of Desire*, p. 3.

12. Herrera, *Border-Crosser with a Lamborghini Dream*, p. 20.

CRITICAL BIBLIOGRAPHY

Bell, Marvin. "A Poet's Sampler: Juan Felipe Herrera." *Boston Review* 14 (October 1989): 6.

Cavallari, Héctor Mario. "La muerte y el deseo: notas sobre la poesía de Juan Felipe Herrera." *Palabra* 4–5 (Spring–Fall 1983): 97–106.

Flores, Lauro H. "Auto-referencialidad y subversión: observaciones (con)textuales en torno a la obra de Juan Felipe Herrera." *Crítica* 2.2 (Fall 1990): 172–81.

———. "Juan Felipe Herrera (1948–)." *Dictionary of Literary Biography: Chicano Writers*. Eds. Francisco A. Lomelí and Carl R. Shirley. Vol. 2. Detroit: Bruccoli Clark Layman Book/Gale Research Inc., 1992. Pp. 137–45.

Foster, Sesshu. "From Logan to the Mission: Riding North through Chicano Literary History with Juan Felipe Herrera." *The Americas Review: A Review of Hispanic Literature and Art of USA* 17.3–4 (Fall 1989): 68–87.

Gaspar de Alba, Alicia. *Chicano Art: Inside/Outside the Master's House*. Austin: University of Texas Press, 1998.

Herrera, Juan Felipe. *Akrílica*. Santa Cruz, CA: Alcatraz Editions, 1989.

———. *Border-Crosser with a Lamborghini Dream*. Tucson: University of Arizona Press, 1999.

———. *Cinnamon Girl: Letters Found Inside a Cereal Box*. New York: Joanna Cotler Books, 2005.

———. *CrashBoomLove: A Novel in Verse*. Albuquerque: University of New Mexico Press, 1999.

———. *Exiles of Desire*. Houston: Arte Público Press, 1985.

———. *Lotería Cards and Fortune Poems: A Book of Lives*. San Francisco: City Lights Books, 1999.

———. *Notebooks of a Chile Verde Smuggler*. Tucson: University of Arizona Press, 2002.

———. *Rebozos of Love/We Have Woven/Sudor de Pueblos/On Our Back*. San Diego: Toltecas en Aztlán Publications, 1974.

Lomelí, Francisco A., and Donaldo W. Urioste. "Herrera, Juan Felipe. *Rebozos of Love/We Have Woven/Sudor de Pueblos/On Our Back*." *Chicano Perspectives in Literature: A Critical and Annotated Bibliography*. Albuquerque: Pajarito Publications, 1976. Pp. 26–27.

Mesa-Bains, Amalia. "Domesticana: The Sensibility of Chicana Rasquache." *Distant Relations*. Ed. Trisha Ziff. New York: Smart Art Press, 1995. Pp. 156–59.

Ortego, Philip D. "The Chicano Renaissance." *Social Casework* 52 (May 1971): 294–307.

Rodríguez, Juan. "El florecimiento de la literatura chicana." *La otra cara de México: El pueblo chicano*. Ed. David Maciel. Mexico City: Ediciones "El Caballito," 1977. Pp. 348–69.

Vaquera-Vásquez, Santiago. "Juan Felipe Herrera (1948–)." *Latino and Latina Writers*. Ed. Alan West-Durán. New York: Charles Scribner's Sons, 2004. Pp. 281–98.

Ybarra-Frausto, Tomás. "Rasquachismo: A Chicano Sensibility." *Chicano Art: Resistance and Affirmation, 1965–1985*. Eds. Richard Griswold del Castillo, Teresa McKenna, and Yvonne Yarbro-Bejarano. Los Angeles: Wight Art Gallery, University of California, Los Angeles, 1991. Pp. 155–62.

A CERTAIN MAN

| EARLY POEMS 1969–1973 |

A Certain Man

The man over there
with educated fingers and fast
    clouds
around his flag
rolls his shirt sleeves & calls
a taxi from church . . .
His eyeteeth clap like his family
for an encore of southwest earth
wolfed with fever
. . . Skilled and styled to believe
that Moctezuma blood & spirit
. . . are dead, as he pumps
a book through his ears.
Inside his stomach
roast meat (buttered in
    philosophy)
makes yellow drops
on his hide overboil down
to his buttons.
Only heavy fur pulls
his head to a pillow
rusting completely overnight
. . . like his prayer.

In the Cannery the Porpoise Soul

In the cannery the porpoise soul
& the shadow fins of spirit boats lie awake
the hundred hooks & flying reels
one harpoon
& the silver fleshing in the nets

the mayor is waiting/counting scales
dreaming new quotas & tuna coasts
(under the table blood & payrolls
swim to the shores on a crucifix of oil)

in the cannery the porpoise soul
steals a dagger for the engines throat
tuna fins etch an X
on the green stone of the ships floor

there are documents with worker sweat
files & rolled sleeve salt
a spear of sails & anchor years
(lost)
inside the shoulders & against the ropes
(somehow)
a policy gunned the waves back
before the porpoise sea was born

Mar 3

Cuántos vientres
van flotando en las olas
cuántas sangres
y campanas de madera
una cruz de san juan apóstol
una rueda de gaviotas en la brisa
quiero quemar el mar
con las minas toscas de un beso
quiero romper las nubes
con una espada de arena y aretes de fuego

Let Me Talk of the Years/500 (L.A. 1969)

Let me talk of the years
years
strung like sweat over nails & bones
years
rung like ancient hooks in the throat of spring
years
torn like oranges over a sidewalk in space
100
blue eyes and white ferns were cast
blue dreams and white centuries were burned
blue flesh was made where once there was only white
blue nails on white coffins were thrown
white
people were chained to swallow blue spears
& white was space turning into red
blood.
200
blue brothers were forgotten
blue deserts were left alone
white flowers meant white jets
& blue rivers never meant white snow
300
let me talk of the years
years pressed like wood
years driven like trains
years
lonely on sidewalks blue with rain
400
i remember caroline
just like i remember juan
i remember broken amber shoulders
& venice drowning in burgundy
i remember endless piers rusting in her golden arms
& the long sea full of doors

& the frozen sky without windows
the burning bones of chrysanthemums
& the hurling flags inside the fence
500
blue eyes & white ferns were forgotten
yet the river smiled
the eagle spoke
blue thunder & black mountains kissed

Gallery of Time

Yesterday the gallery hung
the mustache of zapata
& the look of blood
over walls painted antique white
the compassion of van gogh
sold for a bone of sheep
a coat of smiles
and a brasserie of wine/yesterday
murrieta's head was weighed
& given away with a cocktail
of maraschino red & visceral blue
texas was brought under glass
in a tube of words
(bought aesthetically by a ship of wolves)
a memory now
over cognac & aperitifs of spurs/yesterday
the rhythm of jesus steps
the texture of buddha's eyes
the harmony of tláloc's heart
the oil of vishnu's fire
the balance of moses' serpent staff
auctioned & taken down
& traded
for the opal of herod's dreams
for the throne of mars
for the arms of islands tightly roped
in the cellars of américa

(where they smell of flesh & burning love)

REBOZOS OF LOVE
WE HAVE WOVEN
SUDOR DE PUEBLOS
ON OUR BACK

| 1974 |

[Let Us Gather in a Flourishing Way]

Let us gather in a flourishing way
with sunluz grains abriendo los cantos
que cargamos cada día
en el young pasto nuestro cuerpo
para regalar y dar feliz perlas pearls
of corn flowing árboles de vida en las cuatro esquinas
let us gather in a flourishing way
contentos llenos de fuerza to vida
giving nacimientos to fragrant ríos
dulces frescos verdes turquoise strong
carne de nuestros hijos rainbows
let us gather in a flourishing way
en la luz y en la carne of our heart to toil
tranquilos in fields of blossoms
juntos to stretch los brazos
tranquilos with the rain en la mañana
temprana estrella on our forehead
cielo de calor and wisdom to meet us
where we toil siempre
in the garden of our struggle and joy
let us offer our hearts a saludar our águila rising
freedom
a celebrar woven brazos branches ramas
piedras nopales plumas piercing bursting
figs and aguacates
ripe mariposa fields and mares claros
of our face
to breathe todos en el camino blessing
seeds to give to grow maiztlán
en las manos de nuestro amor

[Quetzalcóatl No Sorrow]

Quetzalcóatl
no sorrow
vida
brillando
quetzalcóatl
plumed heart
of struggle
feliz
laborando
transformando
dying constellations
cycles of thought-action
raw crying sangres
de nuestro señor-señora
life-energy fields
valles
y llanos rojos latiendo
un nuevo orden
terrenal
pulmones punzando
frentes alzando
corazones laborando
quetzalcóatl
rising spiral árbol
tule de vida
ramas de luz
fruto de raza
dulzura en tloque en nahauque
señor-señora
dador de la vida
matriz
entrañas del cosmos de sangres
amerindian fluid

flow ardiente
venas brillantes
corazón consciente
sufriendo
gozando
en la labor
plumed heart struggle
volteando la tierra

[Ipal Nemohuani]

Ipal Nemohuani
raíz de la vida
tú eres el cantor
en el interior de la casa nuestra
en el interior de nuestro cuerpo
en el interior de la tierra nuestra
a   m   e   r   i   n   d   i   a
tú eres el cantor
Ipal Nemohuani
raíz de la vida
se alzan los cantos de los pueblos
como las flores de la primavera se alzan los pueblos de amerindia
como las ramas de la ceiba

[Los chapulines verdes vuelan]

Los chapulines verdes vuelan
el grillo toca su acordeón
raspan sus cantos en el adobe

los campos brillan
la paja 'stá cortada
los pinos crecen alto
el cedro y el piñón
se mecen

corre el agua del ojo viejo
la mariposa
y el cuervo beben el sol
y rajan el viento

"Fíjese señor que ante' era como si fuéramo'
bendecido' por dio'
se te caía una semilla y crecía una flor
los indio' y nojotro' teníamo' fiesta junto'
bajábamo' al río y cojíamo' pescao'

ahora señor
la gente ya no cree ya no cree
las sierras 'stán cercadas
y los rinches cobran pa' pescar en
nuestra mesma tierra que ya muy dura 'stá
que tenemo' que hacer trabajo po' allá
en colorao' en las minas o peleando los fuegos
en los bosques
antes el venadito venía pa' 'bajo del cerro
acá 'tras la casa corriendo libre y alegre
'hora se necesita licencia pa' cazar venao'

por cincuenta dólares la hacen pos'
nomás los texanos la compran
le digo señor era como si fueramo' bendecidos
por dios
asina mero . . . "

Los niños sus brazos castaños cargan leña
la piel de la mujer y el hombre es roja
apretada por el sol viva franca
salada y fecunda

"Vamo' a ver
caminando sin platicar
laborando pa' encontrar nuestra vida
en este llano de soledad
vamo' hacer nuestra labor nuestra oración
el sacrificio sin ambición
caminando sin platicar en este llano
de pasto amarillo por el dolor
vamo' a ver
si vamo' a ser enteros ansina como el amanecer . . . "
enteras y enteros corazón sin fronteras
hopi navajo san juan taos truchas chamizal
picurís pojoaque peñasco velarde amalia y
española piedra lumbre tres ritos las cruces
mesquite tierra amarilla santa fe y albuquerque
santa fuerza vamo' a ser

una luz una oración una labor una nación
la canción sin mirar o decir o medir la memoria
o el mañana
vamo' a ver

nuestros pueblos nuestros rostros y entrañas
soplar en el viento
murmurar en el río
palpitar en el llano
caminar sin platicar

una flor sin fronteras
en el pedregal

[Arizón maricopa tempe tu tierra roja]

arizón
maricopa
tempe tu tierra roja sangre tu vereda
arid sunset sweet
arizón
cactos espigas de espinas
brazos verdes llantos altos
almas ramas pulmones
pizcando el cielo
arizón
campesinos levantando algodón
estrellas de oro blanco pa'l ranchero
nubes de sal
sellos de sueldo pa'l que hace labor
cuerpos rojos
climbing cotton flowers
to the dawn weaving una risa sin dolor
arizón
a las tres de la mañana
hay que rajar la raíz del tiempo
es que
campesinos si nos hay muchos
levantando el cielo por el campo
arizón
pima
xicano
pápago
apache
arizón
no zon nombres

zon rimas y un ritmo
energía de un principio
si nos levantamos campesinos
levantamos cielos por los pueblos
cotton flower suns

[Vamos a cantar]

Vamos a cantar
dice el quetzal
la luz del río
our
voice

EXILES OF DESIRE

| 1983 |

Exiles

and I heard an unending scream piercing nature.
—from the diary of EDVARD MUNCH, *1892*

At the greyhound bus stations, at airports, at silent wharfs
the bodies exit the crafts. Women, men, children; cast out
from the new paradise.

They are not there in the homeland, in Argentina, not there
in Santiago, Chile; never there in Montevideo, Uruguay,
and they are not here

in *America*

They are in exile: a slow scream across a yellow bridge
the jaws stretched, widening, the eyes multiplied into blood
orbits, torn, whirling, spilling between two slopes; the sea, black,
swallowing all prayers, shadeless. Only tall faceless figures
of pain flutter across the bridge. They pace in charred suits,
the hands lift, point and ache and fly at sunset as cold dark
birds. They will hover over the dead ones: a family shattered
by military, buried by hunger, asleep now with the eyes burning
echoes calling *Joaquín, María, Andrea, Joaquín, Joaquín, Andrea,*

en exilio

From here we see them, we the ones from here, not there or across,
only here, without the bridge, without the arms as blue liquid
quenching the secret thirst of unmarked graves, without
our flesh journeying refuge or pilgrimage; not passengers
on imaginary ships sailing between reef and sky, we that die
here awake on Harrison Street, on Excelsior Avenue clutching
the tenderness of chrome radios, whispering to the saints
in supermarkets, motionless in the chasms of playgrounds,
searching at 9 a.m. from our third floor cells, bowing mute,
shoving the curtains with trembling speckled brown hands. Alone,
we look out to the wires, the summer, to the newspapers wound

in knots as matches for tenements. We that look out from
our miniature vestibules, peering out from our old clothes,
the father's well-sewn plaid shirt pocket, an old woman's
oversized wool sweater peering out from the makeshift kitchen.
We peer out to the streets, to the parades, we the ones from here
not there or across, from here, only here. Where is our exile?
Who has taken it?

Black Tenor on Powell Street

Come now, come from where you have stayed in the earth.
—*Tzotzil prayer for calling the soul*

I

Between the St. Francis and
the palms

in the center
between bent mute drivers
on the side

of the last cable car dreaming
to the sky

you sang
from the asphalt altar

in the noon of sirens
and statues

the finger canes of the unbelievers
stabbing the wings

zig-zag seagulls black
notes
from your throat

full of mad choir
spilling on rails
gliding somewhere

bleeding
with the arms thrown
open

reading sunday night riffs
from the Fillmore Gospel

in the Kaos of the silent
bodies rushing.

II

Will you run to the pier?
across Broadway to the sea?

will you leave
the skin torn soprano moon
as you fly?

to the deep green jazz
to the blood sax waves
to the coral tombs of space

will you search
among the pilgrimage
of elder reefs?

whispering
dreaming
pointing

against the city through the fog
your X silhouette

reaching for Malcolm
singing

singing
Malcolm's last Aria
screaming

Return.

Children of Space

I

On Valencia Street the playground aches. Children float through parking lots riddled with the screams of distant throats. Daughter-hands toss the toy over the clouds; invisible. The mother in apartment G gazes, not inhaling. The father coils the fingers around transparent shoulders in the air. Slowly, they undress. Only the stains of the assassinations remain on their bodies. They do not speak now. They cannot speak. Willingly, they have cut something inside. Vowels bleed across the sheets.

II

They enter windows. They exit through small openings. Even their bones are changing. Soon, they will be unable to walk. The two will end in a stance, nude; one pressed against the toilet towel rack, the mirror speckled with images of rapid hands wet. The other hits each fist against the living room wall: please   me/leave   me.

III

In the sunlight the children rotate in soundless collisions, beyond the rented

structures

into an infinite system of undecipherable signs.

The Dreamboxer

His eyes, they slant in exotic ways.
  —*Therese Covarrubias*

(He wakes up, rushes through clothes. He dresses. Leaving the apartment,
leaving the gallery of silent morning rituals, he will penetrate the city;
facing somewhere, some jovial coat, some nude statue, some quick mirage
of shuffling ankles. He will follow the daily exercise of his existence.)

With his hands
the soft
ends of imagination
cutting across
the other face
blood opens
its bell
the sun in the air
rings
through marrow
everywhere
through the fists
and the shoulders
of space.

They are watching
everyone
seated infinitely full
of eyes
wondering
of incest rounds
tossing each other
nude wanting
the grave childhood
of the tracking flesh
open.

They have paid
to see you
your gestures
your signals
how you attack the counterweight
with footwork
how you seek the wet pendulum
of skin.

(He walks toward her body: his church. The stained glass doors are open.
The guards by the holy steps give ointment and the men in procession
are dressing her, baptizing her forehead, drawing her belly tabernacle
criss-cross with tongue and fingernail. They burn boundaries across the
back, thighs, breasts and lips, leaving, perhaps, spaces of the forearms
and neck unmarked. The choir rises, solemn, in the dark boulevard.
The guards kneel, waiting, huddled, murmuring the new obligations . . .
he walks toward the candles in her eyes.)

I will dress you
in textiles and glass
under
an archway of light.

(The body is humming in the distance inside a square. Men-lovers are
leaving with amulets; the breast-forehead, *churchbell of the father*,
the rib-arm, *hovering wand of the son*, the pubis-knee, *bleeding stone
of the mate*. He runs for the body in the center. The shrine must exist.)

(And she spoke)

Am I the figurine
inside the black box?

Who will be
the sparring trickster
the laced-glove killer
against me?

(Inside the coliseum, we sit alone on platforms
we are clutching empty packages. Our heads form
rosaries whispering *we want the prize*. We dream
of a purse dipped in blood, we know, we bet:
we will win. The loser will be the woman painted
on the canvas, lying crucified by our fast craft,
our sacred hate.)

At the Exodus Gym/Valencia Street

Jaime, lift weights. There is no suffering on earth, not even in rooms.
You can feel only metal, white, pure, aluminum, the leather cushions, the hips
churning against the bed structure, silver bricks pulling the legs forward,
cartilages, sinews; the gelatin dies. The arm in the center of the mat,
the arm, alone, hovering by the lights, the fist, the hard father's finger points,
Jaime. The virgin on your arm glows, the gold designs on her veils flutter
sweat, Jaime, there is no moon in this sky, no crescent of light underneath
the Adidas, only a horizon of mirrors, a band of loyal torsos burning
florescent, curling into tight caskets of membrane, breathing out the voiceless
kiss of pain, the handsome smoke of soldiers training, counting the shifts
of eyes, the enemies, practicing alien maneuvers, silently, glaring, bending,
preparing for ambush, stalking in groups of three, registering blood, going fast

to scream forever

in war. Jaime

Module Metropolis

B. Fragment from the Rebellion

It is an island of jugular explosions. A womb
of faceless bees, an armless serum of chaos
spilling out

Pulling the magnetic pulp of stones and glass
the abandoned quartz knives of priests
from the world

Cut open
veins from zone dwellings, petals from boulevard
hair, torn, the midnight suits, acrylic lips
the eyebrow blades, neon tattoos destroyed
with fangs, flowers shriek in venom

Desire drills a sightless bouquet of red knots
curling city compounds of skin, cartridges
of nerves through the fingers and

Incandescent backbones
the trapezius gone into liquid
into pulse only, shadow

Rhythm gliding
going over green fur, wounds, metal play cages
imaginations

Into a journey of unknown triangles or circles or
lines going up, a vapor, a dark swarm of spears.

C. Untitled Note Fragment

Is it possible to be anyone here?

V

The next morning the neighboring renters huddled. The speckled weeds
· remained scattered, some congealing, bending toward unidentifiable
regions of the metropolis.

Soon, the neighbors disappeared in the distance; their shoulders tilting at
    certain angles, their eyes fixed
on the peculiar style of their paradise.

NOTE:

Unfortunately, I am not at liberty to go into more details. The leading
subcommittee of my compound would destroy this account. Already they
have intercepted and received some of the chapters and are announcing
the material as an imaginary story: a series of poems. They are calling it
Module Metropolis. Once it reaches other precincts the title may change,
but undoubtedly it will bear the stamp of the principal officers (please see
attached envelope).

Literary Asylums

for Francisco X. Alarcón & Alfred Arteaga

WRITING

(Writing is richman's work, therefore richman's history. Lately, the unrich are growing accustomed to the forbidden pleasure of writing.)

R-writers live in immense warehouses. There they write at ease; all quarters are at their disposal, anytime. They will summon the workers, the maids. They will call upon the ushers, the watchmen at the snap of a button, the tone of a finger, a casual flutter of an eyebrow or even with a rhythmic twitch of a torso. They are to be served with imagination, magazines, graphic suffering, light-tables, ribbons, rare inks, tall quills. They can dictate, murmur, jump glottal stops, gargle, spit, jam the jaw out, point with the cornea, pin down figures with an opaque thin triangle of elbow for the ecstasy of a thought, a fancy, a dream, a vision (especially a vision) for an ether, a helium space, an infinite image of a new warehouse: a turquoise clinic spinning in the future filled with flasks of dormant immortal replicas, unmixed serums and hexagons: crystals awaiting a genealogy of R-words.

No one needs to hear the saga of the R-writer that rejects the kingdom, that undergoes a series of initiations, that confesses and casts out the jewels from the family's purse heralding verses from the colony of the beasts. There is always an element of suspicion in the claims of all converts. It is said that the beast obeys the master's wish. Even if we grant that animals engage in rational deliberation, a beast must follow the command or meet its death. Perhaps the beast can rehearse loyalty, disguise allegiance while conjuring plans to overtake the household. Perhaps after the overthrow a celebration will mark a new age.

Will they still obey an invisible voice? Will the creatures be able to pronounce the new language? What words? What signs? What writing?

Obviously, unrich writers are not animals, not reptiles. It does not matter. They are prowling at the master's gate. Most are feasting, many have repainted the walls, remodeled the furniture, provided extra exits, taken the mahogany bedroom headboards out, shaken the ivory tusk carved woman away from the staircase entrance, stripped the floors, thrown out the serfs (in most instances). After changing their names they will gather in the same rectangles: the kitchen, the family room, the porch, next to the vegetable gardens admiring native art. Somewhere, in one of the studios, tablets of the ancestors are being placed openly over velvet cushions. There is quiet laughter amidst the ferns.

READING

There are no audiences. No readers. An audience is an assumption, an image: silent flesh block of absorbing membrane. An idea.

Faces have the same diameter of cells across the forehead. Everyone wears shoes, socks, stockings, underwear, shirts, blouses, shoulder pads, cuffs, brassieres, earrings, watches, zippers, buttons, wallets, hats, caps, scarfs, lotions, spray, has 10 fingers, 1 hand folded over the husband's knee, the wife's thigh, the child's neck sitting, the eyes sitting, sitting, the ears, sitting, sitting the belly sitting, the sitting throat, open, listening across the tiers, the warehouse, listening across the floors, wet, clean, listening to the writer read, write, words, reading.

Another idea of audience: the conquered, the unkempt, the wounded, the forgotten, the dreaming, spread over a mat, the boards under blue light, they lay over assemblages of coats, razors. No sofas. They fall back, back to back.

Does it matter?
The idea of an audience, the idea itself cuts into all descriptions, tears into all experience. The assumption of an audience: *they are listening*. That is it. Who listens, if they cannot gain power, if they cannot prevent power from being taken? There are only guards.

No one is talking about handcuffs, wardens, stripes, breaking rock with long hammers. Remember? No one was talking about fangs, claws or foaming fur. It is a simple angle. If you think there is an audience, you don't see guards, the eyes tracking your lips, taking your oxygen away into a hearse, tearing the spine, the skin, off, making splintered bone shoot out with veins as ribbons, as petals for a funeral bouquet. The body lays cut behind camouflaged watchtowers. Nude. You don't see their lapels stained with fluids from your syllables. You see an audience only. You don't listen to the iron gates closing, locking slow around you at every vowel; only audience.

You are only reading.

BEING

Who wants air?
Explosions disturb the quiet talk in the garden, the dining room.
Gas jets of flesh perturb the remote chatter of assemblies in the south quarters. At best, the galleries will stage a false burst of bodies from a cell; a delirium of actors will escape from a gray frame of papier-mâché.

The theater of the unrich will emerge. Applause.

Who wants air?
Who will destroy?

Not hurt, not mutilate, not even assassinate, but, destroy.
Can individuals perform this maneuver? Must there be group consensus?
Has the world ever known destruction or only change?

We are busy at the museums. We are going over and over and over the archives of our own bandages. There are no R-writers. There are no unrich. Even guards really do not exist. There are only bleeding asylums for those that cannot breathe.

Outside beasts and jagged strokes of color blur.

Nightpainters

1

They observe the wounds. Only observance is possible here
in the daylight. At night, they will refigure with the palette
of moonlight, with the turpentine of fever. The brown wound
jutting through the shirt, into the air, will become a circling
nipple at dusk. Jagged streaks across the neck under the black
musk of tropical rain will stream and descend as sweating leaves
across the round and hard canyons. The destroyed backbone, the leg
and its innumerable endings, the mother's belly scorned with bayonets
the child's arms singed in ambush: only ink tracings of the night
being etched on cold ground. They observe. They can no longer
remember. Only observance is possible. They have forgotten their
villages: *San Vicente, Aguilares, Sensuntepeque.* They want these
remembrances; one of them runs and embraces the others, he points
to the distant mountains behind them, his delicate hand hesitates
he is resolute; it is not his village, no more; it is a gallery
of night's work.

2

On the shirt pocket the stain is expanding, slowly, with every village
he passes. Perhaps, tonight, the stain will become a gold medal engraved
with the symbols of the father. They march and observe as they soften
a narrow pathway around the borders of the crop fields; caña shoots
above them, covering their eyes, their medals. They anoint the landscape
with their thin fingers, drawing in the twilight, over the roofs, here
at the mound, facing Las Cabañas, here at the corn harvest surrounding
Morazán. They follow these umber maps with boots and enter. You
can see them from the hills; the uniforms are too silent as they pause
on the side of the municipios.

3

Waiting perched on stones or trees or memories; from here they can see
the teams of bees close by, steadfast, pulling new phrases from yellow
petals, weaving messages with the last edges of daylight. The uniforms
twitch, tear. Their eyes have become as large as the face. The face is
one eye pointing heavy iron rifles, aiming. It is time to design the days
as wounds, to go into the houses and trembling tents and suddenly scatter
the tender chests of unnamed wood, the family letters moist with dreams
and summer, miniature altars guarding a shadow underneath the makeshift
bed, the boards, the green candle vase screaming with its tongue on fire
and through the curtain doors, the dark flight of shrapnel into flesh.
Again, to tear the flesh, the moaning flesh of the giantess' mouth opens
across the village with the abyss in every stone, calling out and echoing
in the black dome of burials growing over the earth.

4

The small band hovers over the body. They gaze at the pool of a bursting
wound, unaware that at morning this body will crush them, these little
soldiers see wounds only, their eyes have been condemned to remain open
forever. That is why at night they will retreat over the horizon and
turn back once again and again they will see their valley of wounds;
this ominous painting mounting over the gallery of mountains,
coming toward them.

War Voyeurs

for Clara Fraser

I do not understand why men make war.

Is it because artillery is the most stoic example
of what flesh can become?
Is it because the military plan is the final map
drawn by the wisest hunter?
Is it because the neutron ray is the invincible finger
no one will disobey?

or

Is it because the flood of blood is the proper penance
workers must pay for failing tribute at the prescribed
hour?

I do not understand why men make war.

Is it because when death is multiple and 'expanding, there
among the odd assemblages, arbitrary and unnamed, there
among the shrivelled mountains, distorted and hollow, there
among the liquid farms and cities, cold and sallow, there
among the splintered bones of children, women, men and cattle
there and only there, the eerie head of power is being born?

Is it because submission is the only gesture to be rehearsed,
to be dressed, to be modeled, to be cast, to be chosen
in the one and only one drama to be staged in the theater of
this world, where everyone must act with the backbone humbled
with the mascara of bondage, with the lipstick of slaves under
the light of gentle assassination with applause piercing the ground
forever?

or

Is it because war is the secret room of all things to be kept
sealed and contained, to be conquered and renamed *woman*
enclosed by an empire of walls, vaults, hinges and locks with
the hot key that men and only men must possess for an eternal
evening to visit and contemplate, to snap open a favorite window
and gaze at the calibrated murder as lovers of beauty?

FACEGAMES

| 1987 |

Cimabue, Goya, Beginnings

I carry a dark necklace around my neck.
It's painted on.

No one has taken notice.

They think it's an outline or an odd shadow.
No one has stared longer than a few seconds.

I'll tell you.

I didn't know where to put all the fragments of the novel
that family never finished. It had such sweet beginnings,
but it grew umber with a onc-eyed madonna hovering
over the lampshade.

So many years, I whispered to her
come to me,
listen to me,
I understand.

She would appear to me with gold-leaf
around her braids and seven daggers erect over the heart;

perhaps the last desires; the first real words
escaping from my grandmother's grave, trying to touch
my hair as I sat at seventeen, writing, inventing her memory.

Her voice was so loving,
now, all that remains is this broken leash
of black sparkles.

Inside the Jacket

I remember, many years ago,
a mexicano working in a sweat shop
on E Street by the library.

I could see him through the window—
a tailor by trade.

Thought about asking him
to make me a suit for graduation.

His fingers were so thin, so dark.

Usually, he labored on a sport coat.
Could tell the owner had granted him
privacy.

He seemed happy and at ease.
One evening, I passed by and gazed
at his finery; his project:

venom lacing
a serpent feverishly winding out of the earth
wrapping around the furniture, into the ceiling,

a gold lacing, swelling,
pouring out into the night,
an iridescent skin, leaping
out of his scarred hands,
spreading across the city.

Crescent Moon on a Cat's Collar

for Alurista

I come from a family of madmen and extravagant women.

My uncle, back in '26
wrote to the president of Mexico.

He accused him of murdering the potato eaters
by the millions.

So, they set him up for life
in a Goddamn Army hospital mental ward.
Another uncle

Xavier Levario got in with big business
making toys out of wood. I could have gone to France,
that's where the art was, he said. But I joined everybody
in the States.

Armanda, my aunt whose hair has always looked like
gold dust,
a fleece,

owned the only swimming pool in the heart of Mexico City
near *la Calle Uruguay.*

My father drove a pink Ford down the main drag in Tijuana.
All the women loved him, no one has ever smiled sweeter.

My pocket is full of ancient coins.
I keep a silver box of African and Zapotec amulets and hair
near my bed, a tarnished sword and acrylics.

Lightning zig-zags like a dog's tail
everytime I throw a stone in Southern Arizona.

I have fallen in wells and risen.
All my enemies, including the governors and the wardens,
keep away from my eyes and especially

from the rhythms swelling up through my feet and out
of the opal triumph of my voice.

Under the Sombrero of Reagan's Coiffure

There is nothing here;
absolute shadow.

A taciturn machine gun
and a secretary lie tangled elsewhere.

(In the office, everyone
has assumed an air of distaste for prophesies,
even if all the oil of all the hinges
is slowly receding to the Arctic.)

Social workers, pool sharks and novelists
have all undergone the prescribed reconstructions.

Everyone has vanished.

Colette predicts a hasty ending
from her loft somewhere
overlooking the bay.

Inferno St.

I am dressed for the occasion.

My lover's torso of enigmatic jade haunts you,
doesn't it?

My grandmother's last wish stalks
the plateaus where the night watchman lives.

Look at me
and the ravenous soldiers I break bread with.

Switchblade,
Little silver boy,
guide me into the multi-night.

My Mother's Coat Is Green

Emerald.
A sea of broken guitars.

Cubism leaning against an old fence
in El Paso, Texas.

No one knows her except me.

Every now and then she plays a fugue in the mansion.
Or she walks on the meadows with all the children,
singing.

Yesterday, she told me age is inevitable.
Then, she spoke of emptiness;

a carpet beneath us,
stray patches of dreams that escape us.

The Man with the Cactus Heart

Political meetings
cabbage and richman's literature
(oh, yes, and altar boys)

abolish them. Immediately.

I want to go to Milano.
Eat chocolate.

You with music—
a crescendo.

These are the principal things;
a condensed century

for my thirst. Reach into me.

I beg you, open this shirt pressing violently,
breathe into me.

Odalisque

s l e n d e r
    e
    p   s
    t h i s t l e   r
    h   a s p e c t s o f a l o v e r
                                         a
                                         d
                                         i
                                         n
                                     going
                                     toward
                                     you inside

Dear Rosinna,
everything is yours now
the apple tree under us all
even this silly script condensing into
language, yesterday, somehow
love and its phosphorescent orbits
burst
pulling the world I held closely and privately
into a void
a black slapstick guitar
on your belly
write me soon.

Movieola

It's about a young generation
whose souls are bombed out.

(You don't need to look for subtlety,
near psychotic material is plentiful.)

Their craftsmanship is superb.

Dear Flakka,

he hit you, repeatedly
because he took you for an actress-mistress.
Think of him now, an undergraduate   e
peeping tom.   n

```
                              e
                              n
                              s
                              o
                              r o s a r y
                              y     r
                                    t
                                    f
                                    l
                                    i
                                    c
                              k i c k
```

Foreign Inhabitant

I have lived here, in exile, for seven years.
There was a trial.

It didn't come to nothing.

The papers said I tried to wrap a wire
around a dignitary's neck. I escaped.
But why do I tell you this?

We are all assassins
coveting the warmth inside the jeweler's castle.
I came to America.

I live in the middle of a commoner's quarters,
underground, with a light-skinned and robust Joe Youknowho,
and the unforgiving squint from an abandoned grandmother
at the end of the hallway.

I stay up at night hearing the crackle of the toaster,
the sizzle of tomatoes with peppers, the President's speech
and on the FM, an old song by Astrid Gilberto.

Write poems and blow smoke rings.
Pull in and feel the scar underneath the left side of my shirt;
it is my wife: smooth, thin, silent, floating, somewhere
around me, far away.

No one obeys the calendar or the clock;
those very loud open-mouthed executioners
of our smallest and secret imaginings.
Not anymore. We go about like the vapor of candles,
attached only to our own whispers.

We hear about suicide squads;
a bomb in the Safeway supermarkets or the Golden Gate.
It's funny, now that I am here,
warmth disappears quickly.
Now, I can say this.

Why did I run from here?
War inevitably opens all the doors.
My people back home must know this.

Only a very few
at the front of the barracks
still believe in the dark blue evening
that will shield us with a star.

AKRÍLICA

| 1989 |

Kaos Beneath the Buttons/Acrylic in Blue

Besides the eternal street corners
the Arab's grocery store across the way
by the building with the antique pianos
the ocean stolen by a little girl
and her smile
rosaries wound on aging fingertips
every night behind the windows
like black clocks pumping incense
his eyes exploded
he
in the dark branches of his room
on the third floor of his winter
began to breathe
even if the sun was to fill with blood
or
even if the uniformed scorpions
were to invent a new makeup/he wanted
everything/everything
even the white rime
on the blind man's cane
the insomnia
of night fruit/the husks and
the legs in the birdbishop's cell
> *you wanted the sidewalk to flood you*
> *cloud music on your skin*
> *you wanted to ignite your lips and your belly*
> *on the wall of invisible women*
beginning to breathe
and to turn the boulevard over with your eyelids
you will embrace two planets in the gaze
of a little girl
you will murder a man under a palm tree
in that apartment
with his modern suit and his shirt wrapped tight
around your body

Kaos debajo de los botones/Akrílica en azul

Además de las esquinas eternas
los abarrotes del árabe contraesquina
con el edificio de pianos antiguos
el mar arrebatado por una niña
y su sonrisa
los rosarios en las yemas ancianas
cada noche detrás de las ventanas
como relojes negros palpitando incienso
los ojos explotaban
él
entre las ramas oscuras de su cuarto
en el tercer piso de su invierno
empezaba a respirar
aunque el sol se llenará de sangre
o
aunque los uniformados alacranes
inventarán un nuevo maquillaje/todo
lo deseaba/todo
hasta la rima blanca en el bastón
del ciego
las ojeras
en la fruta de la noche/las cáscaras y
las piernas en la celda del pájarobispo
    querías inundarte en la banqueta
    las notas de las nubes y tu cintura
    en la pared de mujeres invisibles
empezando a respirar
a voltear el boulevard con tus párpados
abrazarás al hombre debajo de la palmera
en aquel apartamento
con su traje moderno y su camisa ceñida
a tu cuerpo

Suicide in Hollywood

LUPE VÉLEZ (CIRC. 1923)/SERIGRAPH OF A MEXICAN ACTRESS

I visited Lupe Vélez, who was a great figure of the stage and screen,
several times at the Hotel Reforma and in the studios where she was
filming *Zandunga*; she was charming and sometimes I speak of her
with Edelmira Zúñiga, who was her best friend and who brought
her body back to Mexico.
    —*Rafael Solana*, Siempre

the traffic in san juan de letrán cuts beauty marks from blouses sighs
from transparent tires broken pavement the hand of a shoeshine boy
pours grease on soles of tree leather covered with honking horns that smear
shade over a madhouse of hummingbirds
                                        and you're lost in theaters
of tangled legs your stockings running branches of spit and smoke
in the bellies of black ballerinas.
                                        the afternoons are sinking.
clouds wheeling over hungry arrows eyelids
in the rebozo of the girl kneeling beside the ticket booth
                                        the moon oozes
boils up in the breasts of lovers
on the green benches of the Alameda
                                        they're laughing.
                        Lupe
you were left drowned in a toilet the last scene in your throat
facing a little audience of white tiles
                                        lightless
            can you go back to your past?

posters and smiles sadistic extravaganzas and tarzans swinging
among purple veins of your sheets scattered through the streets
                                        dying   for a secret
cosmetic thick with the scent of weeping in yellow vases and cigarettes
burning out in your arms the american sun
shoving the sperm into your brown back and the cashier asking
for dollars so everyone can forget your deathless shoulders
in nocturnal taxis of enamel a monopoly of movies and mirrors
that could never murder your black eyes

The Boy of Seventeen

The boy of seventeen
twists in the sheets
pages of sex
  the bolts are crying
  the windows are crying
his legs sweat camphor
and his blue lips
are dissolved into his cheeks
the pillows' hollows
are withering
  the door is crying
  seeing the keys
  the clock cries
  burning the curtains
the boy of seventeen
a paragraph of rain
between silk and marble
he measures the nails
in Christ's arms
he wants an X
on the left side of his dreams

  he searches for his mother
  naked on the red altar

Quentino

I'm writing you on this ocean table/a paragraph between the sand tablets/a pilgrimage of eyes/from the chasm to the voice/here outside/when someone screams the branches moisten with gray lips and veils/words fly up from the beams of shoulders/and bellies like startled gulls/bellies of prisoner thunder/slave salt/it's Friday Quentino/your 18 years/beat in the cell/like littleboyfists/here too there is an iron tuberculosis/the spider's smile/daggers springing from the nipples of the administrators/secretaries naked in a chainlink shorthand/it's Friday/when the old men are rocking in big dark armchairs and/now and then look at their trembling hands/the jawbones groaning in the pasture/and then/your eyebrows remembered/ and your guitarfists that used to play sun and moon when/we asked only for earth/we're in June/somewhere between the first and the/thirtieth/ Quentino/an infinite petal between two imaginary padlocks/Quentino/and the iodine flag in the soldiers' barracks and the perfume in your hands and the assemblage of an M-16 stuck in Somoza's face?/45 years of smoke and blood exploded in the street/what changes?/Quentino/yesterday your father died under the insecure hospital makeup/today

I walk the streets/I look for eyes/and look for them/I look when it's lighter but the people get used to the eternal/bars/between their eyes and summer

The Secret of My Arms

The secret of my arms
    a bit of gold in the dimness
the course of my blood
    a wing from the sea
the triangle of my roads
    a star of your mouth
the blouse of my guitar
    a stone of gulls
the sketch of my throat
    an oil of your eyes
the flame of my forehead
    a blemish of your tears
the solitude of my hands
    the secret of my arms

El secreto de mis brazos

El secreto de mis brazos
    un oro de la tiniebla
el rumbo de mi sangre
    una ala del mar
el triángulo de mis caminos
    una estrella de tu boca
la blusa de mi guitarra
    una piedra de gaviotas
el dibujo de mi garganta
    un aceite de tus ojos
la flama de mi frente
    un lunar de tu llanto
la soledad de mis manos
    el secreto de mis brazos

Quentino's Journal

Tuesday/January/1979

I write my cousin a few lines, greetings, memories, hugs, periods, words.
I can't ignore the route this letter takes: to San Quentin prison, north
of San Francisco. I read the newspaper. Somoza carries on his bloody
campaign in Nicaragua. I know the FSLN will topple Somoza's throne.
That leaves just one question. How to overthrow Somoza's mind?

In Latin America the difference between the consequences of the oppressor's
ideology and the results of a revolution for liberation is clear. It shines in the
eyes of the peasant, the worker. And is turned into a dark knot of struggle.
In the United States the boss's rage is chanted on channel 7. It's printed on
the covers of records and video cassettes. It's presented in slow motion over
the landscape of a woman's belly pulsing on the screen of our favorite
theater. Its manly scent attracts us. It confesses itself to us in administrative
churches. It greets us in university halls. It showers table manners on us.
It embraces us. It serves us a glass of frigid grins. It unbuttons our suit.
It caresses us, secretly, we surrender and at dusk we begin to build our
own cells. Others (it can't be denied) are guards. Volunteers. It would be
shameful to ask for something, although I have no doubt that groups exist
demanding reimbursement for their hours of service to the state.

The letter will arrive at San Quentin Friday. My cousin will read it.
We'll both realize that the bars separating our worlds are imaginary,
that the free are not free, that prisoners are prisoners.

Monday/April/1979

A few months will pass. The message will arrive that his father is dying.
We'll see each other for the first time in 18 years in a yellowish room
outside the emergency ward in a hospital in San Francisco County. I'll
look at the guard holding my cousin, my cousin beside his fading old
man with plastic tubes up his nose.

Months will pass. We'll hear the news that Somoza is fleeing Nicaragua.
The families, the women, the men, the FSLN, will win.

Sunday/September/1980

In a room in San José my cousin opens the doors. He looks out at the hard, hot avenues. He takes a walk. They'll assassinate Somoza in Paraguay. The motor of his Mercedes will keep running after his body has been blown to bits.

Wednesday/December/1983

On these wide streets, in the parks, in the exclusive shops, in the quiet neighborhood apartments the guards go on, the captives continue. Nobody hears the flashing chains. Why?

Why?

(Note to the reader: I have taken other paragraphs from the Journal *and upon reading them it seems to me that they could be presented in choreographic form. Lately my relations with the person who gave me this manuscript have been tenuous. It's been a while since we've seen each other. I hope this new sketch will be received with refreshed friendship.)*

CONCERNING THE ANTI-THEATER OF *Quentino's Journal*

There are no characters. The group acts collectively and individually to untangle the emotion, the image and the flame of a certain subtle slavery. It's possible to develop direct representations of the text: branches, M-16, seagulls, tuberculosis, secretaries, old folks, grass, padlocks. Or something different can be attempted: gullbranches, oldfolkgrass or grasspadlocks. The essential thing is that the group turns into a metamorphic mineral: secretarypadlockgrass.

The costumes will serve strategically to construct a skin-mural of cold before the public. All will be dressed in various shades of blue and black. The uniform: gray pants, sleeveless shirts and black shoes. The color gray will be smeared under the eyes.

The text of the *Journal* will function flexibly for realizing the work and will simultaneously emerge as a manual for dramatic direction. These two aspects appear as two voices in the *Journal* or one voice with two major tensions. The two will be projected individually and together. The emphasis and the dynamics will be determined by the players. It's necessary that the voice be spread out equally among all, choral at certain moments and fractured and individual at others. The *Journal* contains a thousand voices and one at the same time.

Everything occurs in a single cell. It transpires in a certain city/mind. Time does not exist. Will the *Journal* be an eternal lyric? The voice is darkblue; bearing witness to the constant acceleration of its imprisonment, bearing witness to the growing struggle for its liberation.

The goal of the anti-piece will be to propose to the players, as to the audience, the major part of the work not as actors and spectators but as authors and creators; it defies objectivity, challenges relations; it takes place in the veins, not onstage. Immediacy is poetry; the text, the public; perception, the scenery. In this way the anti-piece and its purpose break loose: creating, sustaining and shooting out a vascular-acoustic-visual electricity; stabbing pains inside the forehead/back; deciphering the impossible; a hoarse sweat on the temples of the universe; the burning ice of the human bars that imprison/lay bare *Quentino's Journal*.

PARAGRAPHS FROM *Quentino's Journal*

Your throat will hum   *I'm writing you on this ocean table*
you'll spin off toward different horizons   *a paragraph between the sand tablets*
kneeling/seated/lying down/crouching
you'll write on invisible iron
on the wall facing the universe
the wall will hum a vertical ocean

You'll seek the eyes with your fingers
you'll walk/you'll run/with frantic
speed/possibly blind/stammering   *a pilgrimage of eyes toward the voice*

You'll have a knot in your throat
the knot will pulse/it will grow/you'll be   *this is where someone shouts*
suffocating/you'll explode in screams

You'll turn yourself into elastic branches
of weeping/grotesque noises will escape
from your mouth   *the branches wet from the filmy*
                                         gray lips

You'll change yourself into a slowly
flying bird

                                         words abandon the timbers of
                                         men and wombs like seagulls taking fright
                                         seagulls of trapped thunder
                                         the enslaved salt

Your body will intertwine with others
you'll moan/you'll go on writing on something
untouchable/hard/you'll sweat/you'll gasp crazily
you'll trap yourself in an invisible box
it will push you/it will press you/with your hands
                                         it's friday quentino
with your fury/you'll beat against that cube *your 18 years in the cells*
                                         beat like littleboyfists
of space/dense

Quickly you'll tie yourself to the others
in a knot/then you'll explode against
the wall/your shoulders
your back/they'll bash/your nails
will scratch the transparent box
slowly/your blood will weaken
you'll sicken/you'll cough/you'll whine/you'll smell
                                         here an iron tuberculosis also exists
like hospitals/you'll be dying

You'll begin to fall apart/suddenly
you'll fall/the others will stay
indifferent/frozen/you'll turn
into a violent skin of bodies
you'll devour the others/the paralyzed ones
you'll swallow them/you'll drown them in laughter

the spider's laugh

The laughter will grow/your skin/animal
of bodies/will begin to spin/fast
it'll burst against the firing-squad wall/
an office wall/typewriter/
men machines/women machines/
administrators and secretaries will hiss *daggers*
springing from the nipples
Over on the wall you'll discover something *of the administrators*
like a calendar/you'll point *the secretaries*
to a particular day *in a chainlink*
you'll duck/machine with delirious *shorthand*
eyes/
you'll pronounce the name in growling
long/high/vanishing voices

it's friday

You'll twist your eyes/slowly/you'll open
a door/you'll grope for the body-chairs/
sitting down you'll become old/you'll drink

a cup of coffee/you won't be able to control

when the old folks rock
your fingers

in big dark chairs and once in awhile
The cup will drop/it'll shatter
you'll kneel looking for it/you won't be able *watch their trembling hands*

| 68

to hold anyone's hand/you'll whine/you'll think about
your useless arms/slowly/you'll force hands
toward your eyes/the howl of the grass will explode

the grass jaws snarl

The grass will sweat a certain cold
you'll squat/you'll look for a cigar
in the bag/you'll search your wallet
for a match/you'll lean into
the light/you'll pick up a photo/
you'll bring it close to your eyes/your hands *and then they'll remember your eyebrows*
will tremble/the photo will slip away *and your guitarfists that played*
you'll grab it in the air/something in your *sun*
hands/will be revived/it'll expand *and*
it'll become something radiant/ *moon*
it'll be a seagull/you'll make it out
disappearing in the sky

when we only asked for earth

You'll lower your head/eyes
you'll walk/lost in triangles
the wall will surprise you/you'll push it
you'll sweat/you'll be determined to knock it down
with your ancient arms/with your veins
you'll burst/
you'll fly/finally you'll be free/
you'll leap/stammering/in happiness you'll hit
others/you'll take off toward the universe *it's june*
a wall will be born/a circular wall/ *somewhere between the first and*
the 30th
it'll compress you into the center of the world

Quentino

You'll drag it a little ways/it'll
press on you/you'll be a prisoner of an   *an infinite petal*
iron blossom/it'll close/it'll open
it will not release you   *between two imaginary locks*

The flower will pulse/it will squeeze/it will oppress
it will hum slow/the buzzing will grow

                                                Quentino
You'll change into a column marching
zig-zag/you'll be a solemn army
with gray banners   *and the iodine flag?*

The columns will advance/they'll join ferociously,
they'll redivide/one will carry M-16 rifles
you'll aim at the others/at the hungry/

                                                between the troops' bedroom
at the stutterers/at the courageous/   *and perfume*

you'll fire

                                                between their hands and the frame
With their rifles/the army will beat   *of an M-16*
on the dead/the army will snarl/
it'll twist/it'll thrust/it'll celebrate
in rage

                                                between Somoza's forehead
Between shrieks of laughter some will begin
to listen/others will smell something in the universe
they'll aim at the darkness/perhaps at someone/
they'll advance slowly/with rifles/they'll follow
growling

"we devote all our efforts
from now on to maintaining
promulgating and defending all
postulates of Somoza's
doctrine
we devote all our efforts
from now on to maintaining
promulgating and defending all
postulates of Somoza's
doctrine"

The dead will wake up/they'll drag themselves along
with their weapons/they'll empty them against the army
they'll kill a few/with rapid fire the army
will finish them all off/except/one will escape
they'll execute her/
you'll awaken from the dead army   *they'll explode in the street*
mourning her in tears   *45 years of smoke and blood*
     Quentino, what changes?
     yesterday your father died
     under the insecure hospital makeup

The others will head off toward different
horizons/kneeling/bent
you'll stay alone/mourning the corpse/you'll feel
a hum in the air/the ones on foot
will moan/frantically they'll repeat fragments/
prayers/you'll abandon the body/
     I walk the streets
the humming will speed up/you'll take a few steps
     I look for eyes and
you'll run after the others
     look for them
     I look when it's lighter

you'll moan/you'll shout/no one will hear you/nobody
the humming will explode/you'll fall to your knees
you'll go on/you'll fall again/you'll scream
the others will pound on the wall of invisible
columns
they'll struggle/they'll smash their weapons against space
they'll bloody their bones/they'll lift their eyes/shoulders

but the people get used to
arms/little by little/they'll hug the wall

they'll curl up/their thighs/their saliva/their breasts
their sleep/their clothes/their suede/on the wall

the eternal bars

they'll kiss it/they'll whisper to it/they'll smile

they'll console themselves/you'll try to free them
you'll shout at them/stammering/you'll throw yourself
at the universe with your arms/open

between their eyes

with your black/dry/eyes
the invisible wall will be humming

and summer.

Exile Boulevard

The dreams are rolling
in broad daylight

after centuries of being arrested
inside a damp room of cheap wood.

The sun beats down on them.

And they keep rolling along and building
new little bedrooms where their small moons
of rage will sleep.

The street is wide.

The supermarket cop prays
his rosary of sighs and keeps track in his notebook
of the sleepwalking eyes floating over the floor.

Tell me Father

what do the pupils of my people confess to you
are they your Sunday collection baskets?

I see
the goat's head wrapped
in a plastic bag

and the short applause
of teeth in its jawbone and it looks at us

and the bag howls and the bodies ignore you
and ask for two pounds of tripe or a few
porkchops and pay their bills

squared off like offerings for a miracle
and they grab the change
and disappear.

Street deep and bitter as hope
scattered between El Salvador and San Francisco.

You carry a scapulary erased by tears
and secret obligations.

Your tattoo of lovers and pilgrimages.

Your earrings of young murder and confetti.

Your belt of Lent and coming out parties.

You smell like a startled womb and healing rituals
at midnight.

At noon
two thousand children march and frown
their first holy communion suit turning
the forehead and opening the tender mouth

forever
forever

forever.

On the corner of 16th they celebrate the wedding
of the commander priest and the woman mayor.

And in all the cells of the tenements
Raul Velasco on channel 14
brings us three young ladies from Nayarit
in Huichol dress and contemporary hairstyles
via all the TV sets

and the spiderweb of wires spinning
above our heads.
Here in the grocery stores
the Mexican bananas murmur.

Hunched-over in their long leopard-skin robes
they slyly point their dark noses
at the poster of Isela Vega.

They are overripe and
the reception was never given

because it's raining and it's time
to leave your teeth with the dentist
and your legs with the surgeon

the clinic
awaits us all.

Street where geraniums shelter newborns
between newspapers, blankets, ashes

and
anise grass and holly.

An old man whose pockets sag with crackers
practices his story for the granddaughter

of vaudeville days
of Cantinflas, Clavillazo and Firulais.

Someone shakes out freshly washed laundry
and hangs it like a crown of bandages
across the roofs and
the steam cries for help and no one listens.

Suddenly a flamenco of laughter explodes
and all you can see through the cracks
are naked backs.

And the ghosts of dishwashers and waitresses
get ready. And the ghosts of candy-makers
come down from the roofs

and up from the basements of the houses
with basins of brown sugar and their kettles
filled with squash

to boil dark mute heads
that twist off alone and decapitate themselves.

And the bakers run down the avenue
with their trays of sharp brilliant offerings
and go into the churches

the movie theaters
and markets and the drugstores
leaving shadows of flour

bread bread
sweet rolls sweet
rolls sweet.

And the time comes for the white streetcar
boarded by its parish of passengers

let's go to the fights
let's go see the champion.

We'll shut the chrome and glass entry
we'll bring dollars and paper streamers

let's go to the fights
the whole family
we'll bet everything

everything
everything.

Who'll drive tonight?

Already the fever of bedrooms and doorways
is flowering

already the cough of the lightbulbs stings.

We'll get away.

I wonder who knows the way?

The sun will come down from its pulpit
with its red
        red
          red cassock

slowly
dissolving
over the boulevard with its open heart.

24th & Autumn

for El Salvador, 1980

I

Will fall be a downpour
of age-old beasts
vanishing
in the wind?

II

Thousands of amputated trunks
below the living room
of the city
continue to bleed bile

the palm trees fan yellow
with blouses of fright
obscuring the songs of birds

all the apartments
resign themselves
to the stairways

under the blows of a stranger's footfalls
going up going down

III

And that man
with lungs

wanting to push
out the whole
plaza

sits down
on a step

to mumble
at the infinite
silence
of the sun

and see
the 17-year-olds who dress in gray
and black

and see
their tough hands and their eyebrows of breeze and smoke
and see

the white electric streetcars screech and stop
at the corner

and open their doors on 24th and Mission

IV

The march that bursts the hoarse flags with fists of sea and
buzzing rages floods the diseased medals the hallucinogenic crowns
the bodies of bright red oxygen who denounce the plague America
the gangrene the Intervention the sores the CIA the pus of
bayonets in El Salvador the mothers with daughters of seven and
twenty Lenten years point at the Junta reclaiming the sleepless volcano
Cuzcatlán to the cotton delirious with the wounded destroying
winter and the sugarcane reborn in the mineral the hour exploding
the lava of the campesinos flowing dark iron with cheeks and
centuries arms and earthquake lips of fire and orange trees burning the universe
raining furrows and flames like honey in combat courageous violent
eternal stars

reviving men and flowers women and suns
among ashes plantations cathedrals and green tombs

V

Does autumn exist?
or just
these last showers
these last graves
thrones and rays
shattering

between summer
and spring?

She Wants the Ring Like He Wants the Suit of Scars/But

She wants the ring like he wants the suit of scars/but

             I

want liquids diamonds from the music of a window when it cracks
cool doors emerald eyes from a fire against ice/everything
screaming torsos petals from an immortal storm
legs of a metallic sea in search of a floor made of fruit
a thousand marias with braids of lightning ruby rifles

                 she wants the ring

like he wants the suit of scars/but

             I

want violetrhymes from the salt mine of a cell when it blows
sky calendars the wall cut by wasp suns

          (cassock wings of altar boys:let them explode)

she wants the ring like he wants the suit of scars/but

                the

one thousand Lucios with honeycomb eyebrows topaz bulletstraps?

Ella quiere el anillo como aquél quiere el traje de la cicatriz/Pero

Ella quiere el anillo como aquél quiere el traje de la cicatriz/pero

yo

quiero líquidos diamantes de la música de una ventana cuando quiebra
puertas frescas esmeraldas ojos de un incendio contra el hielo/todo
que grita torsos pétalos de una piedra inmortal de lluvia
piernas de un metálico mar en busca de un piso de fruta
mil marías con trenzas de relámpago rubí fusiles

ella quiere el anillo

como aquél quiere el traje de la cicatriz/pero

yo

quiero rimasmoradas del salitre de una celda cuando despedaza
calendarios cielos la pared cortada con soles avispas

(sotanas alas de los acólitos:que exploten)

ella quiere el anillo como aquél quiere el traje de la cicatriz/pero

los

mil lucios con cejas de panal topacio carrilleras?

Radio Couples

White streets sanded down by the jawbone afternoon
the chrome muzzle below the leg in the sky/the red
light
the cop in your father chases you glycerine in his navel he loves you
yes dead but the woman of months and insomniac makeup
the mother the young one doesn't know you screams/alone
in a bath of smoke and liquor/she loves you and turns old
you see her
the brother envies you invisible in his car the cathedral silhouette
cold
the doors appear/they open/they want to pronounce you
                c h e n t e
you turn on the gear attached to the fingers
the mouth the throat the breasts the hair
      the harsh skin dark brilliant hard
eyelashes of infinite crystal numbers the curve
the silver back you touch it and it turns murmuring
                e l e c t r i c
in the rain they walk the boulevard slowly happy
                the couple
looking down the alley the foam and metal
                        thinking.

Nuclear Green Night

CHOREO-POEM IN 2 SCENES

VOICES:

The last ones (first voice, second voice, and third voice)
Woman
The voice of the wind
The voice of the sea
The voice of fire
The voice of the sand

SETTING:

(Everything takes place in the ruins of a destroyed metropolis.
The nuclear war is finally over. Only The Last Ones are left,
two men and a woman who meet after having fallen under the rubble.
Near them, within the tangled metal of a building breathes
another woman. Everything is glowing green.)

SCENE I/The Last Ones

We're the last ones. We know it. The rasping metal proclaims it.
All that flows: the oil from blades that were once a luminescent
building of shoulders, glass and offices. We smell the vomit of
asphalt, gypsum, lime and aluminum.

We're trying to decipher our scars. Do we exist? Yes.

There's someone inside the spilled cylinders; the arm splintering
the sky. And the dawns? They don't exist.

Sunrise doesn't exist. Afternoon doesn't exist. The sun itself
is dead. Only the clouds remain. Absolute. Green.

Is this the last shout amid the immense rifts and corpses sinking
in the humid city?

That everyday language, the very breath of family get-togethers, is
dead. Now other signs emerge: the gesture rasping in the

darkness, the sea of deformed neighborhoods, the wind of eyes and
shadows, the fire of delirious dreams and fingers, the sand dressed
in new necklaces; fingernails and wires of flesh.
How do we get back to the beginning, to perfection, to the origin of
our blood,
to paradise new?

*(A woman is perceived in the new darkness. Her breath shivers the skin
of the strangers. She walks alone. She buries the dead world. The
strangers watch her. Nod their heads. They snicker. They know they
are the last ones.)*

We are the last ones. Destruction is our true art.

SCENE II/Testimony

(The Last Ones chase down the walking woman. They stink. They surprise her.)

FIRST VOICE:　How come you're naked in the green night?

SECOND VOICE: She doesn't want to fall in the cylinders
(to itself)

THE WOMAN:　I want to break up the clouds and split the sky
eat the bread of bees
moisten the sun in my mouth
I want to touch the iris of tiny leaves

THIRD VOICE:　The wind is burning the windows and clocks

THE LAST
ONES:　With swords of widowed fire
with asphalt and sulphur clouds

THE VOICE
OF THE WIND: Give the old waves an apple
furious seeds for a grieving womb
give your laugh to the stuttering rocks

a cane for the moon
a rainbow for its throat

SECOND VOICE: Why do you run over the buildings
with your feet of foam?

FIRST VOICE: Why do you bury the streets
the purple hands
the copper voice?

THIRD VOICE: And the hardened blood?

THE VOICE
OF THE SEA: Will you give rifles to the rivers
knives to the ancient seagulls?

THE VOICE
OF FIRE: They've eaten the afternoon in the street
the perfume has been torn from the heart of autumn
the violet has been torn from the green rains
the sky has been torn from the flesh of wheat

THE VOICE
OF THE SAND: Give a daybreak of arms to the shadowed earth
a shawl of fury and a necklace of endless
rebellions

THE WOMAN: For its cold shoulders
for its body of gray doves

THIRD VOICE: Why are you naked in the green night?

THE LAST
ONES: She doesn't want to fall in the cylinders

THE WOMAN: I want to break up the sky and split the clouds
eat bees' bread
moisten the sun in my mouth
I want to touch the iris of the tiny leaves

Arc

Lean your dark back lean
draw a silent arc
exhale slowly exhale
erode my body erode
beneath your breasts beneath
up
up
down slowly down
your hair your beauty marks your sweat
lean your dark back lean

Grafik

for Tomás Mendoza-Harrell & Lauro Flores

I cut / / / / /

I multiply everyday images. I apply an aluminum point.
To the landscape.
To the sentence.
To the photo.
To the figure.
To the word.

And suddenly, with a slight tremor of eyes, vertebrae and fingers, I
destroy everything that exists.

Through the years, I've rebuilt the cells, uncovered the signs of the cold,
immaculate, academic vestibules and of the dead lips and histories in the
metropolitan streets.

My surgery is criminal.

No one has been able to identify the skeletons, the remains, the thousand
scattered nerves of personages I've gathered in order to bring this figure
back to life. The scars are numberless and invisible.

Who would suspect a grafik artist?
Who would suspect this gray table as a chamber of murders?
Instruments:
  — The pencil sleeping with its yellow blanket and rubber crown.
  — A magazine of memories, smiling women, men's suits and watches like
     drops, like science.
  — Tubes of smothered ink sounding like small seas pounding a universe of
     plastic.
  — A photo of a Chamula woman looking through these windows toward
     the Mission.
  — Watercolors: French Ultramarine, Emerald Green and Windsor Violet.
  — Matches thin friends identical soldiers with their red helmets thinking.
  — Dictionaries in Portuguese, Spanish and German, white pages beasts
     nobody hears moaning.

— The priest lantern praying with its head pointing toward the floor in
  front of a fierce wall.
— Solemn archives organized by syllables, breaths, laughs and love with X.
— A book about an artist: *The Fabulous Life of Diego Rivera*, printed in New
  York where they listen to the wind falling from the tallest building.

And the X-acto knives. Triangular. The beautiful blades / / / / /

Every night cars cruise the streets of 24th and Mission. A woman from San
José drives a blue Chevy with smoked windows. Estela. She has reddish
hair. Tight brows and dark eyes desiring everything but this street that
ends in eight blocks: Potrero Avenue. She'll have to turn. But she won't.
She won't go back to the home of twenty years and her father who pretends
to play *Santa* by Agustín Lara on his old guitar and the mother organizing a
Jehovah's Witnesses' meeting. Estela will leave the car parked between
Harrison Street and Alabama in San Francisco. She'll walk aimlessly in the
warmth of the produce stores, into St. Peter's church, by the Galería de la
Raza, China Books, the bakery at La Victoria. She'll walk in the night with
her eyes burning, seeing him laughing, the young man in his black box
apartment, laughing, laughing, laughing like a little man.

The little man laughs. It's an apartment of marriage and fists. The
wife-beater laughs in his easy chair. Next to his bed he sees the anxious
note. He focuses on the signature with the E broken in three places.

He looks at the stained and unmade sheets, the dull curtains, the crushed
cigarettes and the ashes. The black-and-white television announces a sale
of living room furniture. With his can of beer he observes. Smokes. Thinks.

Within a week or two they'll take his cousin to San Quentin prison, again.
The last time he saw him he was a gardener at a college.

He imagines Estela coming home. He imagines and drinks calmly. Makes the
bed. Turns off the television and turns on the fm. He amuses himself in
that space or cube floating above the city.
Estela walks north on the Avenue.

P / O / T / R / E / R / O

Grafiks require precise knives.

> On that day
> When you came to bathe me
> I sweated that stink
> That only the anesthetized
> Can sweat.
>
> You sponged my skin
> Cleaned my hair and
> Seeming to ignore
> My stunned and shriveled genitals
> You nonetheless bathed them . . .
>
> —MICHAEL RAMSEY-PÉREZ

Randi finds himself in a hospital in Los Angeles or maybe further south, in San Diego. I think his parents are from Arizona. He's very ill. He's in a room with a red sign hanging from the doorknob.

I / S / O / L / A / T / I / O / N

His liver is bloated, skin yellowed, hair long and greasy. Weakness consumes him night after night. He can't speak, tires easily. But he can hear. He hears the white heels of the doctors and nurses running to the rooms of the dying. He hears footsteps fluttering like doves over the floor or like the leaves of fever falling from the roof of hell.

It's eleven o'clock at night. He hears the abandoned man in room 200 fall out of bed attempting to drink a glass of water. He hears the IV tubes bursting, the sweet plasma spinning between the walls, the bag slipping to the floor and splattering through the night's open screens.

The man screams. Vomits blood and ulcers. Gets tangled up in sheets and transparent plastic veins. After half an hour doves fly in. The leaves fall. Fast.

After a few days a black man enters room 199. An orderly. He cleans his body with a warm sponge. His hands run slowly down the yellowed back, the belly and fragile shoulders of Randi. Dark birds fly over a forgotten landscape. Randi looks at his mother rubbing his chest with alcohol to quiet the cough before he sleeps. He turns his face. Imagines his one-room house, a trailer his father made out of an old car. They're on a little ranch at the outskirts of an unknown town. The mountains reflect the afternoon's coppery heat. From afar you can see birds crossing above the saguaros and the sky.

The last time I saw Randi was at San Francisco City College. He had just turned in all his papers so he could drop out at midterm. He didn't want to go on with it. It was a farce.

Like when he was invited to read poetry near the Galería de La Raza in the Mission District. He never showed up. Took 18th instead of 24th Street. Some Latinos beat him up. They noticed a homosexual air about him.

Lies do not exist, only the grafik.
This figure has no scars / / / / /

> When I had you they didn't give
> me anything. I grabbed onto the
> washbasin until I thought I'd die
> they did that then. They strapped . . .
> —ALMA LUZ VILLANUEVA

Eva (circa 1946), the doctor says they have to operate. Your pelvis is too narrow. The child can't be born. It will come out in pieces. Eva. They'll have to operate.

He says he'll give you morphine for the stitches afterwards. Even if you scream, Eva, it'll be alright. Even if the nurses ignore you, laugh at you as they see your bluish mouth open, your sleepwalker's eyes, your hands scratching against the metal bed or the air or memories. For one long second they'll study your womb in bandages stains clouds raindrops suns and rouge shadows and rage over the coffin hidden by 10 centimeters of vertical stitching. Eva. You'll hemorrhage 29 days later while washing clothes over a tin basin.

Eva. The doctor is smiling. Have faith in him. He says everything is fine. I've signed the papers. Everything is arranged, girl.

— The pencil wakes
— The sheet tightens, the rubber vibrates
— The magazine fades
— The watch is speechless

Someone has erased all the E's from all the pages; small empty rectangles remain. The ink runs searching for asylum.

— Emerald green is the color of jagged grass
    diluted in great bottles of tears, spit and
    alcohol. It's rain for a hell of cells. They burn
    and burn and burn.

S / I / E / B / R / E / N / N / E / N

Diego, you touch up a colossal worker with too-sad eyes, wearing a faded blue cotton shirt. His eyes are swollen. The worker wants to see, but his eyes don't count anymore, just his hands.
They fly.

They untangle above new machines toward the future. Touching the atmosphere. The fingers touch the 17th of February, 1981.

The National Guard enters the province of Las Cabañas in El Salvador. They trap the area, cutting off all the roads out for the campesinos. Bombs fall. The mountains explode rocks, roots and water. An iron shell splinter rips into the throats of grandfathers and little girls. The initials U S A sweat.

They sweat through the paint of the Guardia helicopters swooping down over the huts and fields of corn.

Seven thousand begin to run toward the Río Lempa. 15km and then the wide river. 15km and then maybe refuge in the jungles of Honduras. Only

15kms
9kms
7kms
6kms   a pregnant young woman disappears
5kms   the Guardia captured her along with the others
4kms   they rip off her clothes
4kms   soldiers in masculine green stained uniforms circle her
4kms   they tie her arms and legs
3kms   the bayonet penetrates

2kms   it etches an x of red tears over the furious womb
6kms   the proud soldier throws down his weapon
12kms sinks his right hand
9kms   rips out the fetus with the fingernails of his hot fingers
13kms lifts it up like a torch
1km   opening his mouth the soldier screams
15kms One less communist in El Salvador!

They reach the river. They jump in the water. Suddenly, from the Honduran side other helicopters and machine guns appear. The wind surrenders. The afternoon weakens.

The giant worker's machinery shrieks on the tiny corner of the page: Plate number 113. It's your self-portrait that you painted on the walls of the San Francisco Art Institute.

Few blades have been needed / / / / /

This time. I used a few blades to fill the canvas with its dramatis personae, landscapes and scenes that have been held back and kept secret; a figure dealt out in different boxes toward different destinies. No one has been able to figure out what happened on this table. But it's time to turn off the black lamp.

If they ask me, I'll do the only thing I can. I'll show them everything
I have; the only thing that counts:

/////////////////////////////OOOOOOOOooooooooooooooooooo////////////

2424242424242424242424242424242424242424242424242424242424242424

februaryfebruaryfebruaryfebruaryfebruaryfebruaryfebr

Circacircacircacircacircacircacircacircacircacirca

AAAAAAAAAAAAAAAAAAAAAAAAAAAAAAAAAAAAAA

15151515151515151515151515151515151515151515151515

brennenbrennenbrennenbrennenbrennenbrennenbrennen

???

fotofotofotofotofotofotofotofotofotofotofotofotofoto

threethousandthreethousandthreethousandthreethousa

iiiiiiiiiiiiiiiiiiiiiiiiiiiiiiiiiiiiiiiiiiiiiiiiiiiiiiiiiiiiiiii

bladebladebladebladebladcbladebladebladebladeblad

potrero//////   /////////   /////   //////   ///   ////   /// //   //potrero

traptraptraptraptraptraptraptraptraptraptraptraptrapt

xxxxxxxxxxxxxxxxxxxxxxxxxxxxxxxxxxxxxxx?xxxxxxxxxx

uuuuuuuuuuuuuuXuuuuuuuu uuuuu uuuu uuuu uuuuuuuuuuu

gre-ngre-ngre-ngre-ngre-ngre-ngre-ngre-ngre-ng

himhimhimhimhimhimhimhimhimhimhimhimhimhimhim

herherherherherherherherherherherherherherherher

....e......................

....e.............................rouge...............

....e................................

leavesleavesleavesleavesleavesleavesleavesleaveslea

pencilpencilpencilpencilpencilpencilpencilpencilpencilpencilpen

usausausausausausausausausausausausausausausausa

riverriverriverL?L?L?L?L?L?L?L?L?L?L?L?L?riverriverriver

- - - - - - - - - - - - - + - - - - - = = = = = = = = = + = = = + = = = = = + - = - - - - - - -

(((((((((((((((((((((((((((#)))))))))))))))))))))))(((((#)))))))))))(#)))

C/////////////R/////////////I/////////////M/////////////E/////////////S

| 94

Gráfika

para Tomás Mendoza-Harrell

Yo corto / / / / /

Multiplico las imágenes cotidianas. Les aplico una punta de aluminio.
Al paisaje.
A la frase.
A la foto.
A la figura.
A la palabra.

Y de repente, con un pequeño sismo de ojos, espinazo y dedos, destrozo todo
lo que existe.

A través de los años he reconstruido las células, desenterrado los signos
de los limpios y fríos vestíbulos de las academias y de los muertos labios
e historias en las calles metropolitanas.

Mi cirugía es criminal.

Nadie ha logrado identificar los esqueletos, los despojos, los desparramados
nervios de los miles personajes que he recogido para revivir esta figura.
Las cicatrices son innumerables e invisibles.

¿Quién sospecharía de un artista gráfiko?
¿Quién sospecharía de esta mesa gris como camarote de asesinatos?
Instrumentos:
  —El lápiz que duerme con su sábana amarilla y su corona de hule;
  —Un magazín de memorias, mujeres sonrientes, trajes masculinos y relojes
    como gotas y ciencia;
  —Tubos de tinta que se asfixia y suena como pequeño mar golpeando un
    universo de plástico blando;
  —Una foto de una mujer Chamula que mira a través de estas ventanas
    hacia el barrio de *La Mission*;
  —Acuarelas de Ultramar Francés, Verde Smeraldo y Violeta Winsor;
  —Cerillos amigos delgados idénticos militares con su casco rojo pensando;

—Diccionarios en portugués, español y alemán páginas blancas bestias que
   nadie oye gemir;
—La lámpara sacerdote de metal que reza con la cabeza inclinada hacia al
   suelo frente a una pared atroz;
—Archivos solemnes organizados por sílabas, suspiros, por risa y amor con X;
—Un libro sobre un artista: *The Fabulous Life of Diego Rivera*; impreso en
   Nueva York donde escuchan al viento caer desde el edificio más alto.

Y las navajas gráfikas. Triangulares. Las hermosas navajas / / / / /

Cada noche los autos cruzan las calles la 24 y La Mission. Una mujer
de San José maneja un Chevy azul con vidrio ahumado. Estela. Tiene pelo
rojizo, cejas apretadas y ojos negros que desean todo menos esta calle
que termina en ocho cuadras: Avenida Potrero. Tendrá que voltear. No
volteará. No regresará a la casa de veinte años y su padre que finge
tocar *Santa* de Agustín Lara en la anciana guitarra y la madre organizando
un mitin para los Testigos de Jehová. Estela dejará el coche estacionado
entre las calles Harrison y Alabama de San Francisco. Caminará sin rumbo
en el calor de las tiendas de abarrotes, en la iglesia de San Pedro, por
la Galería de La Raza, China Books, la panadería La Victoria. Caminará
en la noche con los ojos ardiendo, viéndolo a él reír, al joven en su
apartamento caja negra de risas y risas y risas de hombrecito.

El hombrecito se ríe. Es un apartamento de matrimonio y puños. El golpeador
de mujeres se ríe en su sillón. Al lado de la cama mira la nota de ansias.
Se concentra en la firma con la E rota en tres coyunturas.

Mira las sábanas manchadas y abiertas, las cortinas pardas, los cigarros
machucados y la ceniza. La televisión en blanco y negro anuncia una barata
de muebles de sala. Con su bote de cerveza observa. Fuma. Piensa.

Dentro de una semana o dos se llevarán a su primo a la prisión de San Quentín,
otra vez. La última vez que lo vio trabajaba de jardinero en un colegio.

Se imagina que Estela regresa. Se imagina y bebe tranquilamente. Arregla
la cama. Apaga la televisión y prende el fm. Se divierte en aquel espacio
o cubo que flota sobre la ciudad. Estela camina el Norte de la Avenida.

P / O / T / R / E / R / O /

La gráfika requiere sutiles navajas.

> On that day
> When you came to bathe me
> I sweated that stink
> That only the anesthetized
> can sweat.
>
> You sponged my skin
> Cleaned my hair and
> Seeming to ignore
> My stunned and shrivelled genitals
> You nontheless bathed them . . .
> —MICHAEL RAMSEY-PÉREZ

Randi se encuentra en un hospital en Los Angeles o quizás más al Sur, en San Diego. Creo que sus padres son de Arizona. Se encuentra muy grave. Está en un cuarto con un letrero rojo colgando de la agarradera de la puerta:

I / S / O / L / A / T / I / O / N

Tiene el hígado hinchado, la piel amarilla, el cabello aceitoso y largo. La debilidad lo consume noche tras noche. No puede hablar, se cansa. Solamente puede oír. Escucha a los blancos talones de los médicos y las enfermeras correr hacia las salas de los moribundos. Oye las suelas revolotear como palomas sobre el piso o como hojas de fiebre desprendiéndose del techo del infierno.

Son las once de la noche. Oye al hombre abandonado en el cuarto 200 caerse de la cama al intentar tomarse un vaso de agua. Oye romperse los tubos con el suero que penetran las venas. Oye la bolsa de líquido dulce girar entre las paredes, resbalar en el piso y desparramarse por las limpias pantallas de la noche.

El hombre grita. Vomita sangre y úlceras. Se enreda entre sábanas y venas plásticas transparentes. Después de media hora llegan las palomas. Caen las hojas. Veloces.

Después de unos días entra un hombre negro al cuarto 199. Es enfermero.
Le lava el cuerpo con una esponja tibia. Sus manos corren despacio
por la amarillenta espalda, por el vientre y los hombros frágiles de Randi.
Pájaros oscuros vuelan sobre un paisaje olvidado. Randi mira a su madre
frotándole el pecho con alcohol antes de dormir para quitarle la tos.
Voltea la cara. Divisa su casa de un solo cuarto; una traila que hizo
su padre de un carro viejo. Están en un ranchito a las orillas de un pueblo
desconocido. Las montañas relumbran el calor y cobre de la tarde. De lejos
se pueden ver unas aves cruzando los saguaros y el firmamento.

La última vez que vi a Randi fue en San Francisco City College. Acababa de
entregar todos los papeles necesarios para salirse a medio año. No quiso
seguir. Fue una farsa.

Como cuando los invitaron a leer poesía cerca de la Galería de La Raza en
el barrio de La Mission. Nunca llegó. Tomó la calle 18 en vez de la 24.
Lo golpearon unos latinos. Le notaron un aire de homosexual.

No existen las mentiras, únicamente la gráfika.
Esta figura no tiene cicatrices / / / / /

> When I had you they didn't give
> me anything. I grabbed onto the
> washbasin until I thought I'd die
> they did that then. They strapped . . .
> —ALMA LUZ VILLANUEVA

Eva (circa 1946) el doctor dice que es necesario operarte. Tu pelvis
está muy chica. La criatura no podrá nacer. Saldrá a pedazos. Eva. Tendrá
que operarte.

Dice que después te darán morfina para el dolor de las puntadas. Aunque
grites, Eva, todo estará bien. Aunque las enfermeras te ignoren, te ridiculicen
al ver tu boca abierta morada, tus ojos sonámbulos, las manos rasguñando
el metal de la cama o el aire o las memorias. Por un segundo infinito

contemplarán tu vientre con vendas manchas nubes gotas soles y sombras de
rouge y rabia sobre el sepulcro oculto por diez centímetros de costura
vertical. Eva. Te dará una hemorragia en veintinueve días al estar
lavando ropa sobre una tina de hojalata.

Eva. El doctor se está sonriendo. Ten fe en él. Dice que todo está bien.
Ya firmé las papeles. Ya está todo arreglado, muchacha.

— El lápiz se despierta
— La sábana se aprieta, el hule vibra
— El magazín se tiñe
— El reloj está mudo

Alguien ha eliminado todas las E's de todas las páginas; quedan pequeños
rectángulos vacíos. La tinta escurre buscando asilo.

— Verde Smeraldo es el color de un filoso zacate diluido
   en grandes botellas de lágrimas, saliva y alcohol. Es lluvia
   para un infierno de células. Arden y arden y arden.

S / I / E / B / R / E / N / N / E / N

Diego, retocas a un obrero gigante con los ojos demasiado tristes, con
una camisa de un débil algodón azul. Tiene los ojos hinchados. El obrero
quiere ver, pero los ojos ya no son importantes, sólo las manos.
Vuelan.

Se desenvuelven sobre máquinas nuevas hacia el futuro. Tientan la atmósfera.
Con los dedos tientan el 17 de febrero de 1981.

La Guardia Nacional entra al Departamento de Las Cabañas de El Salvador.
Hacen un *cerco* alrededor de un municipio, cortándoles todos los caminos
de salida a los campesinos. Caen las bombas. Las montañas explotan piedras,
raíces y agua. Una astilla de hierro se clava en las gargantas de los
abuelos y las niñas. Las iniciales U S A sudan.

Sudan debajo de la lámina pintada de los helicópteros de la Guardia.
Descienden sobre las casuchas y los files de maíz.

Siete mil empiezan a correr hacia el Río Lempa. 15 kms y luego el río
ancho. 15 kms y luego quizás refugio en las selvas de Honduras. Solamente

15kms

9kms

7kms

6kms   una joven embarazada desaparece

5kms   la Guardia la tiene sujeta con otros

4kms   le rompen los trapos que viste

4kms   soldados de masculino traje verde y manchas la rodean

4kms   le amarran los brazos y las piernas

3kms   la bayoneta penetra

2kms   raya una X de rojas lágrimas sobre el vientre de furia

6kms   el orgulloso soldado tira el arma a la tierra

12kms   hunde su mano derecha

9kms   arranca el feto con las uñas de los dedos calientes

13kms   lo levanta como antorcha

1km   abre la boca el soldado y grita

15kms   ¡Un comunista menos en El Salvador!

Llegan al río. Se tiran al agua. De repente, por el lado de Honduras aparecen
otros helicópteros y ametralladoras. El viento se rinde. La tarde se gasta.

La máquina del gigante obrero rechina en la pequeña esquina de la página:
lámina número 113. Es tu autorretrato que pintaste en las paredes del
Instituto de Bellas Artes de San Francisco.

Pocas navajas han sido necesarias. / / / / /

Esta vez. Utilicé pocas navajas para poblar este lienzo con personajes,
paisajes y escenarios que han sido detenidos y secretos; figura repartida
en diferentes cajas hacia diferentes destinos. Nadie se ha dado cuenta
de lo que ha sucedido sobre esta mesa. Es hora de apagar la lámpara negra.

Si me preguntan algo, haré lo único que puedo hacer. Les mostraré todo lo que tengo; lo único que cuenta:

/////////////////////////////OOOOOOOOOoooooooooooooooooo/////////////
2424242424242424242424242424242424242424242424242424242424242424
febrerofebrerofebrerofebrerofebrerofebrerofebrerofebrerofebrero
Circacircacircacircacircacircacircacircacircacirca
AAAAAAAAAAAAAAAAAAAAAAAAAAAAAAAAAAAAAAAAAAAAAAAAAAA
151515151515151515151515151515151515151515151515151515151515
brennenbrennenbrennenbrennenbrennenbrennenbrennen
??
fotofotofotofotofotofotofotofotofotofotofotofoto
tresmiltresmiltresmiltresmiltresmiltresmiltresmil
iiiiiiiiiiiiiiiiiiiiiiiiiiiiiiiiiiiiiiiiiiiiiiiiiiiiiiiiiiiiii
navajanavajanavajanavajanavajanavajanavajanavaja
potrero///potrero
cercocercocercocercocercocercocercocercocercocerco
xxxxxxxxxxxxxxxxxxxxxxxxxxxxxxx?xxxxxxxxxxxxxxxxxx
uuuuuuuuuuuuuuuuuuuXuuuuuuuuuuuuuuuuuuuuuuuuuuuuuu
v−rdev−rdev−rdev−rdev−rdev−rdev−rdev−rdev−rdev−rde v
élélélélélélélélélélélélélélélélélélélélélélélél
éllaéllaéllaéllaéllaéllaéllaéllaéllaéllaéllaélla
. . . . e . . . .
. . . . e . . . . rouge . . . .
hojashojashojashojashojashojashojashojashojas
lápizlápizlápizlápizlápizlápizlápizlápizlápiz
usausausausausausausausausausausausausausausa
ríoríoríoríoríoríoríoL?L?L?L?L?L?L?L?L?L?ríoríoríorío
--------------+-----+===========+====+=====+====+======-=-=-
(((((((((((((((((((((#))))))))))))))))))(((#)))))))))))))(#)))))
C///////R///////I///////M///////E///////N///////E///////S

NIGHT TRAIN TO TUXTLA

| 1994 |

Night Train to Tuxtla

The heavens above me
black clouds blending with the white ones.
—*Margarita Luna Robles*

Downslope, sleek concrete.

Blurred gate at La Central in D.F. This is where you bring your bags and
cardboard, leave behind a sack of viscera. It's not going to help you cross
over. La Central: the wooden hub of brown exiles dressed in rubber;
bound south. Some prefer the East. Prefer the South where you can
breathe in broken pieces of sweat music. Billie Holiday and her velveteen
dress waves from above, frocked in a Virgen de Guadalupe shawl. Stars,
marimbas, sex, and moon shafts. She drops it on the man ahead of me, the
guy with a herringbone comb in his hip pocket, the guy, with a newspaper
jammed in his short sport coat, flying. We are all running. No one looks up
toward Billie nude and coming softly with her arms open and her mouth
singing her last song. We think it's behind the windows. The ruffled heat
under our collars, inside the T-shirt. An old woman in a jersey print leaps
through an aisle and grabs a seat. Three students roll into each other and
press through the angled doors dropping books and a canteen full of vodka
and grape soda. Before I get there, the train fills. Jump in, a tiny woman
screams, and I crash on the crooked floor with the rest of the band. The
night explodes and the wheels churn in the rain. The old woman has curled
a giant ball out of rags and presses it into her stomach, bows her head. The
man next to me with his back facing me says his name is Macedonio. He
corrects me and says it's Colonel Macedonio. Worked the sugar mills in
Veracruz for twenty years, got cancer in the liver. Just back from *la clínica*
in D.F., he says. We exchange a few sighs and elbow each other for air. The
storm presses against the glass. The black veins squirm and the moist steel
and plastic leather rock us to sleep. My wife, says another. She left. Didn't
want to make love one afternoon; she called me a thief, rented an old
Cadillac and took off for Morelia. The next day a white kitten in the yard
knocked down a slab of plywood and smashed its own head, it wanted to
live, for a while. Macedonio laughs. He's got his money wound in his socks.

Glass socks he mumbles, bought them at the San Antonio bazaar. A man with a little green suitcase pulled them out, twisted them and lit one up with a match. Then, he stabbed it with a stiletto. Glass, he said. When will we get to Tuxtla? One of the students dressed in Adidas jogging pants says the best shopping malls are in Tuxtla—Gala, Gala, she whispers the name of the place to her girlfriend. We are headed downward. Going into a deeper spin. A darker sleeve of the ocean where the steel wheels turn into sea anemones and the conductor speaks a dolphin language. We are all floating in the mid-levels of the waters, holding each other hand in hand, except my hands can't feel the fingers. Something fluttering and porous is at the end of my right foot. Fall in, into a skull-shaped pit at the bottom. There is a bottom now. A crescent of starfish at the edges play with a bulbous growth. Can barely see. They are building a new hotel in Tuxtla too. *Fiesta Americana*, the girlfriend whispers back. After you leave the station you can feel it as you come into town. On the hill. And the Indian soldiers stand with their automatics. Upright, chromed. At the entrance to every boutique.

Tatarema

The bones curve out from the shoulders
into the earth walls, passages, fifty thousand workers,
sugary discs carried on the back, absent among the shrouds,
only stones, stones upon skull with a thin sheath,

a black hive, Sierra Pelada
gold mines, unforgivable skin, Brazilian,
and there are mouths again, up

through the sod, the broad-hipped caves in the hill, a factory,
a vein-digging chasm, hospitals with old women in torn muslin,
the kind you see in dreams, scorched, greenish, shredded,
this shawl—

in Sertão de Bahia, the 24-year-old bride scratches the back of a rock,
sits in a '61 Rambler station wagon slammed by a truck, engine on,
overlooking the vanishing road, overlooking the sand, chalk dust

on her cheekbone, she wears
a white carnation and the ribbon unwinds on her knees,
ship-breakers,

coal-burning roofers, I am calling you, with your transport—
the heavy steel gash from Bangladesh, remember Bangladesh,

back in '71 someone cried for you,
hailed you and sang to you, I call again, naked without a hat,
if you wander

without a leg long enough, someone will find you and meet you
at the milpa with a Holy Crane–shaped cloud above you, the left hand up
as if holding a witch's white veil,

uncovering the dead of the church, disinheritance—to say it for once,
even if in this text, even if your eyes are hard, eating cold,

from the dented steel bowl, with a shadowy spoon,
with your hands at the waist at the end of the sugarcane day
cutting the rust from your night face,

come with a beard, with a shirt rolled and a fist wrapped,
and a stream of banana leaf and the feet with a barbed pick in the earth,
I am not describing the subject,

this is not the subject, dear reader, the ceramic baby in shards,
not skin anymore, kneeling again, again, yes—kneeling
at the handmade canal,

bricks without milk and the woman's bosom
wrapped in a hotel blanket left long ago,

a Bush maid under contract again, with the belly
streaming, coal soot and penniless, the hearth beaten down to the tin,
it is not unusual,

it is not unusual to write this,
remember that if you wish,

there is a wicker basket with a stone balanced on the head, a cotton plant
splayed against the air—history, someone says, this is how you learn to walk,
there is a canvas waiting for you, yes, for you,

the dunes, the white shroud I spoke of,
an olive cut open inside the eye and the hand waving
good-bye, tied to a wire,

a medical chart for tuberculosis—refugee, you,
say it—refugee in a camp against the tree full of triumph over you,
that cactus with loud courage over you, too, claws and shadows
again (so many shadows), two men praying—in their seventies,

wearing white again, also a soiled gurney floats
against the side wall of the village, woven by hand, perhaps
the children passing time, thinking of the sea—

one body at a time, here is the triumph you were asking for,
a gunnysack, knotted, muslin again, this spotted film the body wears
when it is flayed, there's a junkyard lacking wood, a steering wheel
shoots up from the heap, a mother wants it for her child,

maybe it will roll to heaven, maybe it will turn to music,
then flies, a loaf of bread and then, a city—for once,

a shaft inside the bluish rock, jutting its face into a fender, halfway,
tombstones made of coral and a boy thinking like this,

like this, yes—in a room, alone, thatched roof again, crosshatched by the
Sun Gods it is said, tied up the to the ankle, the boy's own camouflage from
himself—leprosy, he wanders, too, in this half-light, inside the closets,

the child half into the woman,
her legs stretched out against the Coptic floor,
an Ethiopian dispensary, yes, in a different shape from ours,
another shroud,

a warehouse of shrouds this time, empty, bitten sand, coffee cans,
tents, ten thousand pushing against the Korean mountain, big-bodied
women and men, oblong, they hear about food,

so they march, with a cane shoot and a folded rubber sack,
folded at the knuckles, shaving the skin—for a moment, the children pose
for a burial ceremony, the wheeze of the elders rises,

one shows her buck teeth, hiding behind a jagged slate
Sertão de Paraiba and crisscross the forehead, with the eyes
up in half-moon,

lost, holy Tarahumaras, speaking a word or two, famished, coppery
by the twig house, a child, again,

with candy-colored yarns in her hair, another marriage—think of this,
another marriage in the yards,

the man with a labyrinth tie and a game on the inside floor,
a bone game for the Great Wars—Tatarema—about to come,

what will protect you?
Open your arms

as if diving into leaves, the grave, the parted rag door in your house,
and the Holy Spirit on the last days of the year, dovelike, crosslike

with a jawbone and a healing stick above the lattice,
there is a bus stop, too, in Huautla de Jiménez,

two withered dogs lying on a flour sack, empty, slates again, a candle,
a vase with an explosion of black and the caress of a child, a boy this time
on the way to a carnival,

there is a delivery to the village, a visit to the blind aunt,
a reddish patch that must be healed, a blanket of tiny rocks
and a violin, thick necked, festive,

an open gate of wooden trunks caught upside down,
emptying a few dance skirts, a military cap, in the back yards,

two boys and a girl with a palm leaf on her head,
ready for burial—looking steadily

now, yes—only now
there is time for that,

the cactus winds up its hair, glistens for a second
inside the spine, the oxen taste the plow and the mineral mountain
slips back into the wound,

the pewter mine in Oruro, Bolivia, the men unshaven
with their hands hidden from each other, three women dancing,
a tuba with a gaping lung, blue and black, a red screen,

a vapor, again, curling, and a clarinet on the table,
it is so still, so cold, this table where the mason and the wind carve a rose,
then, the glance of the dead goat, the flowers, tiny
oval tortillas and the chicken, headless over a colored pastel plate—

the eyelids, stretched, again, almost oiled,
clouds with their mother faces turned toward us, the mother

infested with crazy, moving lines above the brow and her melting eyes,
holding, reaching, mantislike, she wears a hat, too,

a boiling tin pot held up by a weight scale for oranges, pushing
through the God sounds,

fifty thousand Indians, you could call them all
and they would turn to you and they would point with clay stub arms,
a dingy shoe, leaning against a single plank, almost a cross, a hull
for a boat used for welding,

according to a plan, determined, overdetermined
by the engineers, wait, don't let that word—engineers—guide you here,
it is meaningless, better say electrical cables, a furnace,

always a furnace in a brown room with goggles or with a dog
abandoning the village, the highest regions across the horizon, uncertain,
graceful, camera-like.

One Is for Maáx, One Is for Jabalí

for the people of Najá village,
Lacandón Rain Forest, Chiapas, México

This unknown fountain. Fifteen Mayas
from Lacanjá. Two from the village of Najá.

The wind on black print tunics. Designs
from the new mestizo factory.

They sit here,
by my knees, in wetness.

A last pin still turns the threads and speaks
for the useful water inside my broken cup.

One of them carries a chrome radio, clings
to the numbers: 5, 6, 7, 8, 9, 9, he leans, he sings

Pixán
Pixán

for tomato
for heart.

An ambush gives them away. I can't tell
if it was yesterday or centuries ago—
blood liquor,

Protestant oils, cheap perfume on the red beans
of the night necklace.

They keep to themselves when they carry this.
They touch a dying bird and speak of the color green.

My blood is this color,
with a full jaw, they say.
I can resist them. I run back to my
anguish and repel the heat, the cotton beak of the sky
comes to face me and I deny it.

The Lacandón Maya boys swing their legs
to one side, to the side of vastness and genocide.

No banquets
on their swollen glands,

the voluptuous mouth of Chan K'in José
as he stands near la Ruta Maya, new road
to the Pemex oil plant, a few miles northwest

up the hill
where the lorry drops Tzeltal Indians.

In their rose skins, with machetes
they dig for the last *caoba* seed, they pull cans and glass.
By the ledge, underneath *la tiendita*

young Nuk sells bloated whips of sugar
and aspirin. She dissolves behind a ragged curtain.
Chan K'in José, in the back, chips and smoothes
a stone point.

He feels the swiftness of the flecked edge;
because the sky brings me secrets
from the trees, he says.

And everyone listens
with love and fullness, a scar on the blue ground.

At midnight, with straight bamboo,
one meter. Wound with smoke wax string,
the arrows are ready.

One is for Maáx, for Howler Monkey.
One is for Jabalí, for deceiving boar.

They will come alone
to your walkway, near the parched stones of Palenque,
waveless, half of the world in light.

Memoria(s)

> Crucé la frontera cargada de dignidad.
> —*Rigoberta Menchú*

It took me long to walk
to this slate, a desert star,
pinned on my forehead, here,
in this brilliant stone rail,
carrying what was given
in sand and pouches
with all my familiars, in rough
kinship, occupied
without a returning spring,
through the sandal bones,

in puzzles, the quake-lined crops,
the picker songs, the passport designed on the neck,
the citizen language,
I speak of Genesis

between my mother and me, between my father
and me,
tear gas gauze, supplications
and her tiny ancient voices

and his long biblical compassions, factories
of dislodged pigments, blue muslin settlements,
a Moroccan tarp
through the short sickle years, the portioned
tomato days, the sliced sugar-cans
in the yard, left
with the imprint of six interrogators,
the doomed pellets
in the hourglass, working the wicked man's yard,
scrubbing and praying

in bone through the village bowl,
all night singing Yemeni songs falling astute
inside the floor, with the knees mapped,

my mother in
her apron condemned, my father
in his long coat of dust,
in his Turkish *baglame* shuffle, a sigh without
the tragedy of passage, this honorable wicker hat,
this merciful Jerusalem open hand, this dead

contract on the shoulders to the skull fields,
to the circular concrete, three columns of army jeeps,
the acrid sweetness at the center,
a mother hand waving,

a slanted apartment, number nine, number four,
number 14,
number this, number again, with salt, with blood
in tins with lost brine, from the last to the first pay stub,
counterclockwise

with the hands in, occupied,
with the house up in shock,

a bread roll behind the back, through the crazy sod,
in the tyrannical bar, a child with a meager landscape,
in the match basement
with all my wonderings, in patches,

red, green, and black, without the cloud colors,
without the vowel for an *A*,

for an *E*,
for *E*,
for *U*,
for *O*,
oval for oval sky,

to hang against the petty bureaucrats,
a poor-girl oasis, reflected

at night, to hold in the proud cell, in the eye,
in the ragged arm, her riddled back upright,
his squatted back
upright, your father through the tawdry rope,
through the gnarled vine, the hook knife,
the piece of rain pasted,
a raisin held in the fist, a razor bread, listen,
if you get out

as a night stranger, if you get out face first
there will be air and tobacco, then sing of Istanbul
and Old Jaffa, sweat on the skin,

air, reddish seeds and a ghost full of kinship,
a potter's wheel and a mason's table,
a few friends,
all in a concrete circle, broken or healed, a wound
from the tin boot and a chin strap reflected,
the stub writing,

the short ceiling, the cabbage soup,
a crash of blue maize
in the skillet, in the icebox bundle, my shadow,
my indigo wire,
full of sayings, thirteen days of crucifixions,
in a child's mad combat, the village heart

in the cloth, wrapped, something
about you, something about us, about
this sediment heat, terrible
in its long scarf, in its counterclockwise sheets,
a sky flame and an ash trumpet, caught
on the street sign,

an isolated unit, one last smoke,
tear gas in the coffee cans,
the eyes full of love and a newspaper stabbed
in the mouth, a knife in the shape of a tunnel,
where there is a bag of acorns for the road
ahead, black tea,

I am walking, like this,
in an oval, broken,

cloud healed, in the match gallery,
the canvas is nailed
in shrapnel turquoise and black,
exiles with a short coat,
a torn pocket, spilling salt, into the truck stop dune,
into the scrub rumble, in the short tin,
getting back,
getting out, the reflected soup,
rope questions
in the ancient marrow, in the bone shoot,

inside the trousers,
this dress with wings, so I curl it, caught
in a blue-redness water bucket, so,
I touch it, inside the territories, occupied,
waiting for *mojo*, inside
the *brujería*, the dance-top falling,
thirteen years old and Egyptian,
soon there's water into a flask, with lips,
with a portrait inside the locket, inside
the captain's engine game,
a tyrant's politeness breathes like this

driving me and you,
through the town alley, with the ass scalded,
a factory whistles in bright steam,

this trembling lamb up the official stairs,
was it compassion, was it my generation, was it
there I cried, where I
opened your hand in mine, where I lost
what I had,
and left it, in fullness and amusement,
at the next century by itself, what

I could not keep, what I could not speak,
what I could not remember, it was you,
it was green and red,

walking up to the mosque, three columns of army jeeps,
in arduous light carrying a young boy, in the jaw, awake

he was in white, with tattoos open
in the name of Abraham, in cuneiform,
for years I was hearing the strings ask me
for a grenade

and the short woman, his mother pressed
with tender knives,
so she could protect herself, they were shrunken
flowers and ashes, a cassette by Parisa
unwinding outside
in the tiny brown tent, the brown watchtowers
in full bloom,
he knew this, this jet weight,
a circular concrete,

when he was grown, it was you,
what I could not remember, was it
Ishmael, or Lucia,
a bit to the left, I left you under the olive tree,
outstretched, a lost code spoiling
from your nightshirt, lime

and rot in Gaza, bloodied, shredded,
where children played by the fountain,
their three fingers pointed,
into darkness, into you,

thirteen years
and the darkness swells down, to their little knees,
to this chair hemorrhaging, in the belly,

newborn in a sack of tear gas
and a pocket hinged
with rocks, the first word in Arabic, this
revolving ocelot clock,

this Jewish Olmec face, in the sliced sun, hidden
microphones, ragged, with the skin of millions, with

a trace of a jade shrapnel, a familiar torture
with the filament, inside the eye, the green into black,
the river-sequined boats, the fire blouse,
in the army night,
there is a bird call, the tiny hands of the iris
in the open road, reaching up,
to the village trumpet,
an old woman in the beggar coat, she is
ready for you,

she is listening with a sweetness, at the center,
a heat from a lagoon in Galicia,
in the shape of my mother,
of your ghost father, without a hat,
a blue coat wing,
this time, out of the boot grave,
out of the wire,

the dim passport from Cairo, the hidden wooden slate,
slashed twice, this sweat justice,
this tombstone ice,

this beat to the riff, reddish, for a petty bureaucrat
collar broken, over the galloping breast, over

the moon saga, in exodus, there we clap
for an amused sail, coming up,
through the potatoes and rifles, the singing mandible,
the lightness of Istanbul and Old Jaffa, the hull
that unwinds, the rust breath from the shirt pocket,
this fever hypnosis, this slash in the leg,

I walk through
the sharpness, this greenish flask in the hoping shoe,
I come to you, now, I bring this,
only for you, what I left behind,
was it the dawn-eyed village alley,
the intrepid nets of hushed camps, you

with your embarcation, gypsy-Indian hair, and me
without a hat, did you love me, walking behind,
mumbling, digging through Palestine, finding myself
in a wooden rice bowl,

in Spanish broken, a carved *baglame*, upside down,
getting it all, never, they said, never, the tyrants

in flashing suits, I was dead dead
in the fish barrel, in the giant despot cheese wheel,
at the leaning
marketplace, in the tent house,
over you, grayish,
full of rain and lost strings,
and outside, an occupied smell lingers
the rubble office,

two interrogators
with a paper bag of sweet rolls, open,
where we begged, where we saw the waves
behind the olives coming up in razor shapes,

up, over the city,
and the shore full of peasants, my mother carrying
a handsome clock, ticking violins,

the lucid bomb, as in her name, for the mumbling
watchtowers, three columns of army jeeps,
in full dress, our embarcation dripping,
telling the story, studying from the oil lamp
with a sweetness at the center, a jade knot,

an Olmec figurine, clay cast in a shadow,
a briefcase in cuneiform, Egyptian, loud in shrubbery,

shreds, in the tall washer kitchen,
in the hollering closet, in this springtime ankle, tied
to innumerable beings, their hands
clutching ancient discs of sugar and bread
and a wooden spoon, this beggar's Mesopotamia
from the invisible, from

the middle of an unknown forest, beginning with the letters
of an *A* and an *L*, and Arabic *F* and an African *Q*
and a Jewish *M* and a Spanish *H*
and an Egyptian *Z* and a killer's *Z* and
another tyrant's *Z*,
with its beginning pointed and its end pointed,
toward you, toward Istanbul and Old Jaffa,
toward this enigmatic net,

this trouser bag, the torso
out of the spoon, in the braided hair unfolding,
ironically, a tiny scream, reddish,

a pomegranate string-bass beat, another riff
from the open tabla,
all of it, just you and me,
the reflected inspector's coat, the night wing
train wheels to Cairo
and then New York, full of stolen conversations,
a tiny encyclopedia of stars, over
the embroidered mosque, below the ice stairs,
under the flower vase, this earthen flask,

full of wonderings, the swollen ships,
the healer's touch inside the exiled liquid,
in the secret thigh, in the arm holding you,

it was you,
tattooed to a tear gas sign,
it was me and the open window, without a nurse,
going counterclockwise eating dust,
a collection of occupied doorways, after
my own white shadow, the sun in spirals,
on your tattered dress, going into
a perfumed peasant's sword, a laughing insomnia,

innumerable beings, tied to my ankles,
dancing on this asphalt slip, this *cante jondo* train,
whistling through the chasm,

the sweetness at the center, the flannel shirt pocket
made in Lebanon, sewn in Tel Aviv,
with your hand in mine and your face against mine,
again, dance skirts and military caps,
the moon broken and full of amusement, the
stringed air, this frozen patch,
green then red then black, the gleaming coffin,
our continental color gone wild,

a number out of the slave shadows, a number
out of an *L*,
another *L*,
an *L* for last,
very last beggar-worker,
the long long step through the factory yard,
the Southern tent hush, the
crop picker standstill, bread rolls and tobacco

carried secretly through the camps,
in the whipping afternoon, gnashing the engines,
the tractor lifting up the bones of the others, buried
in the sweet sod, with their funny handkerchiefs,

an occupied smell, the hard
cheekbones of dead soldiers, without cloud colors,
and the glance of the singing mother,
still on their tiny heads, wrapped in wetness,
this concrete circle, behind the lost,
hushed numbers without a map for lightness,
the hungry towers stealing my bread,
the love of a woman waving, of a man quivering,
an animal caught in the grasses,

looking up at a crazy star, broken
and upright, going and coming, going and coming,

she wants it said, he wants it said,
soothing, and bluish, reddish, string music and
sweet rolls, behind the stairs,

the passport caught in a foreign bosom, the lagoon in
a boot shape, familiar, it is just desire, they said,
emptiness, fullness, once again, terrible breeze
under the lost door of the petty bureaucrat,
a factory office lightbulb,

they feed it and they keep the glistening doorknob,
tight with confessions, they know,
they listen, the strings are going, by themselves,
calling my name, your name hangs
in the cloud air, my father walks alone, again,
and my mother walks next to him,
and she is alone too, and I am here, inside,
with them, it's what you want, it's
in your dress pockets, so much time
through the hourglass, dragging my name,
in cupboard pellets, in the howling silence,
bowing she cannot be seen,
there is something about this, I want to say it,
I want to tell you with words, in kabbala,
the reddish truck

behind the guards, the army opus over you,
cut in half by a jeep, by a masterful stroke
of the driver, learned at night,
the rebel waters peering, taking note,
with skin from our diaries,

I remember all the names,
in cuneiform, the infinite sand walks, dim raceways,
a ship's floor, in the coastal caves,
in the tropical sergeant's cabin, winding,
splintered

a shredded city, rub it,
with prayer and a healer's animal,
a woman with weight calls,
and you will see, with this flask
full of hard coffee, with the Arabic door
and the Hebrew shoe, both banging and burning,
in the moon afternoon sprung open, cast it,

cast it again,
an escapee's spell without a cassock
or an alphabet, the tyrant's silver bites back,
only an open shirt pocket, a sworn word,
to guide you, a golden wheel in promise
across the night train,

the chicken fields full of eyes,
the washer woman wax, the jutting robe of the dead count,

so familiar, a shape concentric, left over,
outstretched in Jerusalem, in something like Kurdish
in a flask, an Egyptian shoe,
for holy walks and night tellings, in wonder,
the village rings,

now, to you, I bring them,
to her, the nameless one with my name, to us, inside,
it took this long, pinned on my forehead,
full of burnished beings, the ones I was given.

City Paint

Reddish flared patches cover our soft houses, our streets.
A wanton perfume seems to pour, thicken these summery decks.
I play cards with a stranger. I pick at secret sentiments. I spin
little pictures for the heart—at anyone's gestured request.

The businessman going north is my guest or I am
asked by others in less formal attire. (I know this—
their ill-freedom gives them away.) A young sailor smokes
a cigarette, a sailor with the lips chafed, chalk marked.

Too much desire, I tell him. The military are marching
as ever. I take stock of these frayed moments. I think
as a clown; the shadowy Mexican kind, leaning jagged
in marketplace air, believing his purplish sparrow puppet.

I linger with an ache, always. Still, I laugh, axe shaped
inside, a Jack of resentments—raised from a trailer
where I was born. Things give me away: my uncle's death—
uncle Geno who cared for my mother as a child. Pure color.

The colors pull me. Somber green blueness. But everyone
stays lithe, somehow. Jugglers of the boulevard, powdered.
We never talk about this, this age. Costumes, disguises.
The evils of the frozen glance stop me, hold me again.

I sit on the park benches. I listen. People look this way;
the left side of the face, darkened. The left angle
of their little rooms falling—one side of the bed pushing
away from their spotted bodies. This is what stops me.

I relax. Stroll into the used bookstores. Astutely
they notice the sections I walk in: Adolescent Literature,
Life magazines cut with thin blue razors. This is how I live
taking note of temperatures, plump forearms loosening.

I'll tell you where I live. An off-white bridge sprayed
with lovers' frenzies leads to my cottage. Under the dull
shield of cement—rafters rattle—men and women hunched,
sitting on their roped boxes. I know this gallery too; gold

leaf torsos glazed in Renaissance promise. Everyone here
gambles on this river shore, goes up the moss mounds
into town, carries a fish pail—waits in line for loaves, aces.
You turn an ivy gate. For a while you talk to the barber

about your little girl and then you mention the curative
powers of the ocean. It is best to gather it in a house jar,
my father used to say. Drink it and it will heal you. Outside
my front window the amber stumps groan; how copper

strips and blurs across these flat planes of the factories.
I read these signs every day. I keep them in my sketch book.
Sometimes I fold them in my pockets. I tap my fingers
there. Let me tell you more about this city. The Victorian

houses are opaque, religious, swollen spires. It is
in the kitchens where people sleep. I never see anyone
walk out or gaze up to lift a windowpane. The second
floor is too weak now. A white shroud covers the stairs.

The shroud falls on the streets too. It seems to comfort
their souls; everyone rests this way, huddled by their
bright yellow stoves. Fire spokes twist as so many years
in the boiling clocks. Then, the docks; hazel, ancient piers;

bitten shore lamps, hollow singing boats, strafed stones,
violet smoke. The muffled music in the reefs calls me.
People pass by—they name me John. They cross their arms
at the rails remembering their crumbled countries;

the parchment map they followed, rust knives they met.
I see them praying for open sable woods, drinking from
the baroque fountains, whispering to lost ones, telling
their grown sons to forgive them, to write soon. I play.

I toss kings from a distance. Sometimes I bring my
ribboned guitar and sing Mexican riddles. Tell of Plácido,
the crazy man who collected brooms so he could build
a ladder to the sky. In other quarters I am a rogue dancer.

Hotels are my favorite theaters. I sway my long tattered
dinner coat, I make people laugh. My red cap shaped as
a canoe; amuse them—the olive fragrance, a burst of memory
makes them see other things: a man with his black gloves,

his lover's letter upstairs in the vestibule. Look at him
smile. I pirouette with Gerard the headwaiter, Carla
the hostess with chocolates—her puffed white legs. Then
we laugh again, nibble. No one points to the resolute

woman about to sever her romance—coffee and penitence,
she says. He says, sugar, two please. I've kept all this
in my journals. Napkins are perfect artifacts. They are left
in flight or ecstasy. I weigh them for signs, for lives.

I stalk the square. I snap blisters, the ochre finish
of abandoned storefront walls. You can scale old rooftops,
feel the braille of end pipes jutting, or archways where
water collects on pebbled ceilings. There is heat, steam.

Below—the library, hot, caged; so still with a woman
inspired. Her pencil elegant, feverish. Husbands thumb
the newspapers, too quickly. Their wives remember them
talking, a curl in their eyes. Desire again, a mark of rage.

With one or two fingers they unravel the well-sewn locks
of their brilliant hair. Nights; I find men confessing in game
parlors; no crucifix. A Caravaggio, drunk by the coin machine
just revolves, pulls his stained, solemn collar. Tomorrow

at the porch; the knees will fold in consolations. Look
across the lawn to the perfect greenness. Daytime
bathes their knuckles; a family album opens. Hands rise
slowly to cup the mouth—a picture is measured, adored.

A few newcomers circle the downtown alleys and arcades
where old beggars with large coat pockets and the young
ones with soft hands sit back on tin gallons, a chipped fire
hydrant. A tiny comedian puffs from the makeshift stage.

Open cream jars on patio chairs, drinks. A whipping taxi
changes gears; a rouge scarf. The knitted stars of a night lamp
spill on the stoic curb. With the late evening radio I hum
over my wedge-table, tap royal faces under the filtered light.

Norteamérica, I Am Your Scar

> Get out of my walled infinity
> of the star circle round my heart.
> —*Vasko Popa*

My friends grab at their shoulders
at odd times. So do I.

There is something eating at the ligaments.

We crouch as if in a snow blizzard.
A stranger's blue wool weighs on us.

And somehow, we still lift
our delicate fingers;
a true gentleness moves.

Our portraits hang on the precipice.

A crazy quill left
for an old woman's barbed hook
undulates inside the small of our back.

It is hard to walk, like this.

It makes us sullen, silent,
with rough lips dying from madness but,
then, our hair that refuses to stop growing
pounds its black tubing into the sea,

excavating,
making room for a forest or
a desert of terrible ink.

And there we sing, at last;
a fang with lightning;

a half-sun breaking from the second story of a tidal wave;
this unfinished stone fist novel unraveling all its wetness.
A quarry knife
I carry, for you. You take it now.
It grows slowly,
inside, an echoing razor, flutelike in a Midwest bar

in Davenport called El Charro,
or Lee Choy's or Fry's Grill on Dubuque Street.

But, you don't see this,
you say you are campaigning.
I received the champagne bottle and the bow tie.

You said everything is ready
and that everyone, even Alma Guttenberger,
the librarian at Haines Hall,
will finally see the color green, beginning emerald.

Here, you say,
take it:

a green saxophone, a scream leashed,
held against our chest.

Inhale
exhale.

And see how our undershirts, our poor fishing skirts tear
and the trouser pocket shoots a wishbone, a toothpick, something
that we've kept for ourselves.

You see, this is what we have;
all we have. You know this.

Your hand bleeds, and the blood smashes onto our roofs
like a reconnaissance map. Or is it our bile?

We are so tied to you. Our hind leg
limps with the cadence of all your daylight thefts
when you leave our yards
with our small icebox under your arm.

We know how you have taken our fender.
How you have lured our dishrag.
How you have hammered
our almond-eyed typewriter ribbon.
We see how you polish your claws.

This is my village, full of crosses, swollen, dedicated to your industry,
groomed in your spirit of bank flowers and helicopter prowls.

I want to say good-bye Big Man.
I want to say farewell Holy Jaw.

But you see, there is very little left to do, now,
except go to the park and relax with you; take your hand
in the shape of my hand

and point with the powdery grace of night,
point to the phosphor crescent on your palm, this scar
you say you got from hunting wild game

somewhere in the South, when you used to dream
about saguaro and when you towered over
the wire coils across the endless borders
and military bridges into my anguish,
into my resentments.

I point there because you will find me
in a shape so familiar, so close to you;

in your language, in your checkered English neckties,
in your translucence and your innumerable notes of ash
and penitence; I point there, you

strong man with a sanguine palm tree leaf
jutting from the robes you wear. The ones we make
with our daily smoke of washerwoman wax.

Listen to me.
Your scar speaks to you.

Your dreams know the scar very well,
there, the scar lives with its bulbous velvet root on fire.
Let's walk together, in this light.

Tonight there will be an animal fair
somewhere in this curled-up nation.
Look there.

This is the age of the half-men
and the half-women.

I say to you, now, I celebrate
when we shall walk with two legs once again
and when our hands shall burst from your hands.

Fuselage Installation

for Scotland

(My loved ones drift into nothingness
—with little red gifts still
in their anxious arms. Little shirts.)

Blaze, the missile shards; your fuselage glitter, stuttered
over the wild crazed mountains; a blast at the exact interval
when coffee was being served. On the last plate,
a frayed napkin casts a claw shadow.

Lift. The hill with little people—tardy saints. Kneel.
They are your lecturers, your gloomed witnesses
with elongated hats; alarming
scarves blossom from their torsos.

The fuselage is—the child, her back mandril blue.
What stone amphitheater sings, what peasant trumpets glare for her?
This dragon vestment is all we have, now: nameless quills,
unknown fins, burning gauze without candlewicks.

You assemble new artillery, set up a helmet monument
inevitably, you salute with pleasure. We follow
in this dome—your basilica of quiet blood. This is your kingdom,
earthquake light.

Penance? Go there
to the waters of the glazed city. All the electric fish, whitened,
loosened from their tarnished silver boots—the ones they used
to bully you.

They too float above your hand, eerie
their purple smoke mouths, triumphant.

Writing by the Hand

for Marvin Bell

According to the pen, the writer was sitting
in an office space—a dense cube. Air and light;
shredding thoughts, the tiny darkened scarf
jutting out from the fingertips. An indigo.
Of course, it wasn't a scarf. As I opened
the fountain—my tongue reached the opaque
film in language. Chain. Coagulation. A call
came in from behind, an attempt to give
selfless love—only the spirit bestows it;
waves from the spirit-light as it bounces
out from the shirt. Then, the desk flipping
an ace of diamonds from the thumb: a reason,
one more milliliter of longing—a baby wink
for Mother Jasmine. The pen was taciturn
yet, busy, very busy stabbing the rubbery mat
under the arm; this soft sponge plenum.
You have to admit that this is ridiculous,
Pedro Towers thought as he pressed on;
the fountain was very busy. Pedro was staring
at the little snarls of indigo leaves. Who
was Mother Jasmine? Does she have the maps
to the fountain? Is she a fictitious card figure?
Why is this pen blending so well into the film?
Can the bluish waters lead to other tables
beyond language? Unassembled, crying. Still.
Laughing out loud? A mischievous Dante in New
York, for example. The arm so fastened. Elbows,
so devout. Every follicle on the epithelium bends,
sways again. In some uncanny way, things
are going awry; the fountain suggests this.
Pedro wishes to celebrate in a particular zone.
Away with brain-shadows, he says. No more.

Pedro, a man about town, about country, feels
(yes, feels) that everything is false, now.
This blackish mat hiding under the wrists; this
is disappearing, he says. A nothing-blue.
Lies. Below him. He must try to capture
what happened earlier—according to the box
in the room. There is a germ nosing up:
his will, of course; memories, potentials,
dances—signs left on this side. Not enough
for the pen to go down. In the end, Pedro
Towers must contract a fever—a Paradiso
shell glowing within the shirt pocket.
Timeless. Whatever articulations he invents
will be yours. Myth and coffee, Jasmine or milk.

The Sea During Springtime

for Aurelia Quintana, RIP, & Francis Wong

Come down to this stony day
—an evening when I lift my head.

Gaze at the architecture,
greenish, sealed.

Peasant shadows and hours pour from my skin.
It isn't a burial mound I am looking at.

It is lost beneath the lead and wood
and the angles of my pressing mouth.

I cannot drink from its tides.
It is a sea that will open in another sky.

There is only a white tiger
pacing beneath the black.

Designs inside my bones.
Aurelia Quintana is dead.

Laundry faith woman, solitary soup overseer
in an oven for holy brooms.

I circle her from a distance
in el Valle de San Joaquín.

My uncle lifts her from a candlelike bench
shaped by silence and his captive soul.

My aunt smells of plants tonight—lavish,
thick lipped, wet, spinning in the jade center.

More shadows, embossed,
carved with my solemn left hand.

The burnisher that I keep is well defined and alive.
I earn this knife from dirt and apartment lamps.

I earn the kerosene and accordion smoke.
Once my mother hid there while she was kissing.

Once I wept there and saw my father leave.
He was leaving the same way we left every city.

Now my spirit pushes me toward the tower.
No one is there—except my grandfather, Alejo.

He is the man who cut maguey,
pulled the whitish juice from a pointed heart.

He is the worker who turned to salt. Pulque
down the arms. A tiny soul slobbering birth.

I am carrying the dead. I can hear them
nibble my ears with their faint tongues.

Late hours—a spirit sits on my head.
Then it throws my legs to one side.

I raise my hand and grab the night air,
silvery in its grain.

Silvery in its oceans. Silvery
in its feminine voices.

You never visited.
You walked the streams.

When you told me, singing
I saw your dead child.

He was locked away, beneath
Briars and merciless woods.

After he fell,
No one looked for him.

And now?
And now?

The waters are yellow and blue by the trail,
reflecting the oval sky.

A boat rushes with women, men and children.
Dark hair and swaying torsos.

An old man with a reddish beard stands
alone by the sails, laughing.

He asks me to cross this bluish bridge
where people lean over and gaze.

A watercolor of green and shredded violet
comes to light my face again.

There are gulls in the air. A black hat.
Carnations, crescent disks. Prayer.

A little battle for heat. Naked
without a jacket, grayish. I give thanks.

My belly is deep into the sod. A baby boy
in cottons and a pomegranate flush calls me too.

Three steps above me. Two roses above his head,
bowed. He is also a wheel of concentric infinities.

I can place my tears on his round arms.
I can place my death on his shoulders.

Above the ground, in my stupor
—this is the way I walk.

A black pagoda comes up through the waves.
I am full of beginnings. I am full of wonderings.

String music. Mussels and sea bark.
Clams as flint and pursed as castanets.

An open palm inside. Aurelia leans
by the grasses. Her legs cross the sands.

Aurelia pulls at her rings and shawls,
soft and earthen. We dance in a full circle.

Around the coral. She steps into a wider ring.
Water washes my feet, goes up to my navel.

Another wave thrashes the satin arm of my spirit.
I am ready to sing. My aunt Aurelia weeps.

Aurelia sits on a parchment—
the one my mother carried since she was a girl.

It is made of fibers and leaves gathered on the way.
She is young. She is restless and slides down a rock.

Her hair long—going. Snow and sunlight
in the winds. It is springtime.

It must be springtime in the mountains
where the sea begins.

Iowa Blues Bar Spiritual

Little Tokyo bar—

ladies night, smoky gauze balcony, whispering. Tommy Becker,
makes up words to "La Bamba"—request by Hard Jackson,

mechanic on the left side of Paulie, oldies dancer, glowing
with everything inside of her, shattered remembrances, healed

in lavender nail polish, the jagged fingernail tapping. So
play it hard above this floor, this velvet desert. I want

the Titian ochre yeast of winter, keyboard man, fix your eyes
on my eyes and tell me, handsome, how long will I live?

How many double-fisted desires, crushed letters, will I lift
in this terrain? And this rumbling sleeve, this ironed flint

of inquisitions and imaginary executors, where shall I strike,
what proud stones? Will this fauna open for me, ever, this fuzz,

anointed beak inside the bartender's mirrors, etched doves,
a cautious spiral Harley tank, hissing, this Indian bead choker on Rita's neck?

How long shall we remain as wavy reflections,
imitators of our own jacket's frown? Who shall awaken first?

Margo Fitzer, the waitress? I will say, Queen Margo, sing to me
stoic princess of slavering hearts, three faint lines creased

on your satin belly, toss our planet onto your umber lacquer tray,
too empty now; make the earth spin its dog rhapsody, erotic

through this silvery off-ramp and flake, unfurl. We tumble across
this raceway in honey-glazed traces, our arms ahead, the hands

flying to Ricky's Ice Cream Parlour, outside. I want to own one
someday, maybe on Thirty-Second Street. You will see me

in my gelled waved hair, my busy wrists—so fast, a clown's
resolute gloves, dipping faster than finger painting—except

I'd be stirring milk and the chocolate foam of love, churning,
burning this sweet spirit, more uncertain, than the celestial

sheaths above the prairie frost. See the boy coming, they chide,
leaning, how he crosses his legs, his eyes dreaming, sideburns

just shaved clean. He weighs the sour slate on his father's breath;
perfume, fortune, cards left on the bleeding table. Milo Wilkens, drummer

at the curve, strokes his nipples with his arms as he hits the high hat.
Somewhere in the back rooms, I know, a shrine, orange sponge cushions,

two toilets and a wire wound wicker box, to leave flowers, occasional
offerings by the Johnson County dudes, detasselers in jersey ties.

Talk no more, enjoy. Darling singer, let your starry blouse sway me,
steal this fresh peach half from its amber juice; I want the moon

in this nectar, too. The flashing cymbals, feverish. Who can strike
a votive candle, love, or sleep in this electronic night? Just listen

to the two-part harmony, laughter, peeling beyond the cemetery, beyond
the Iowa river—where the spike hat rooster bristles his tiny ears,

bows his head, and sips from the dark canister under the carved pearl-stone.
And then, returns. Let us drink, salute the bright spokes of meal, the dying

wands of river blossoms, grandmother's sacred hair; listen, her soprano
owl, her bluish melody, so thin. Another glass please, we shall dance

once again, our eyebrows smearing against each other's cheekbones, loud
with a Midwest sweat, a cantata from the crosshatch amp, click it.

Click it, for wild kind rain, forgiving seasons, for the blushed bread
of our shoulders and thighs, this night, everyone is here. Even Jeff Yoder

came all the way from Illinois, to fill a bucket with passion, ruffled,
thick. O sax player with a jail needle tattoo, leap onto this wet pavement,

call my lonesome tempest heart, its buried mother's kiss, bless us
in staccato, with quivers of oak branch greenness, and sparrow longings

riff over this brutal sky, give us your bell filled, conjure your tropic,
our lover's breath. Blues bar dancers, jangling gold popcorn, chord makers,

opal-eyed Suzie in a flannel shirt; we beckon the spark, the flaring
this lost body to live.

Alligator

for Matt Lippmann

On the alligator's back
viola tenderness, dark diamond

roses.
Pedro Towers sleeps.

Concrete palisade, blue mystery
his rough tears;

wine to drink. I walk
up to the furniture market, oblong
liver,

madness bloated—the steeple.

In my hurried coat, in parsley night print—
green phosphor

lamps, the heavens
must part. Without love?

The gaunt clock, kabbala—ticking.
At what hours, brothers,

O sisters,
can you tell me?

At the Town Pump on 16th,
the speckled wino's fist
burns without

a wise thumb—lost
on a basketball bet.
Smoke draped,

etched, hardened; luster
of garlic robust whiteness,

bleached face. I go.
I want to bring my father home
now. Clarinet

voice, long coat. Blessed naked leaves
in his pocket. Sing

for his blue coat wing.
Who

will bake bread now, caress
ferns, drag forward the dust at the gate?

Alligator
Alligator eat

my tiny tree heart, ringed
rugola, rugola.

I will grow stronger. Taste
the yellowed herbs, your wild
eyes. I will strike

these dwellings—convex cushions,
shiny toy chests: drops, academies.

Towers Lake thickens; stillness,
fury. He sleeps now,
wet—a handkerchief, the forest

symphony.
He dreams the crumbled recipe,

tangled—sweet:
Apples, raisins,
cinnamon,

lightning—an embarkation, spice.
Rest a little, rest now, you

rise again.

Letter to the Hungry Students of Berlin

> A reclamation of order, re-
> Visioning solace: the great body
> Not torn apart, though raked and raked
> By our claws—
> —*Denise Levertov, "From a Plane," in* The Freeing of the Dust

Big sky, above us.
Yes, above us,
above our flame-scented hair locks,
early and rebellious; the bluish dome casts down
—iciness,
unperturbed, without shadows.
The seduction of the asylum guard is attractive.
We've seen his military clinic, in rubble.
Nourishments,
behind the strings of the enamel cabinets.
Lines of *Asylanten*—refuge seekers
—tiny yellow stamped vials handled so
gently by the old Kommissars.
I smell licorice and turpentine.
Yes, today: this big sky,
tied close to our narrow chests.
We could almost say *the blue-green in the air.*
The blue-green in the air.
Orphaned alcohol spilled by strange gods.
Gifts from the unspeakable convex void.
The Goddess of Tempests and
New Brain Blood welcomes us.
I say this with caution and carelessness.
What is upon us?
What courses through our knock-knees?
Our bright hands of worker soap,
coffee and *Käsekuchen.*
Our rouged knuckles,

—steadfast now
in their reddish corduroy skin.
Look—we bear the flag of rouged knuckles. Yes,
we have a flag now, a skin flag.
Whose flag? Remember the Jewish-skin lamps?
They still burn, inside.
We are the skin lamps now,
at each subway station. In trampled asphalt fields,
wired clay, webbed neon leaves.
Listen,
a tiny watery bulb-heart. Late
under the moon wind,
another autumn, it sings—ocean rage.
Who will touch our new faces, a green
branch held close to our shirts? A book of bread.
Ochre yeast on our lips, blushed with anise.
This bitter-sweet taste of cleanliness, I mean
the wild cleanliness after the avalanche.
Yes, the big sky.
Unfathomable. Our equation.
Who will decipher it?

Listen again:

Dark migrations.
Swiveled currents, disengaged rivers.
Curled fog, dark basso profundo,
in our name, yes, in our broken syllables
for sky
—a lifeboat sails with our voices.
Vigilant, spiritual.
Rising, settling.
What can I lift up
—rippled, enigmatic distances
blown-out daughters and sons?

Mothers, fathers; gone now,
to another age. Dug in, dug out in their humble straight
coats and dissident prayers.
My own mother, Lucia.
She would come out of her second-story
apartment in San Francisco, arm in arm
with my light-haired aunt, Teresa.
In the fifties. Together, go and drink
a cup of coffee—downtown canteens
where Mexican women were not allowed.
My mother
—walked where revolution gets tangled
in the skin and turns into a journey,
into the question of existence, vastness.
In the evening, in velvet solar heat,
we shall meet. On the same fallen granite.
I use that word *granite*.
Maybe in afternoon twilight, talk
in that typical fast manner of yours. You tell me
of the handsome gang onslaughts. Subway glass
smashed with Vietnamese blood. I tell you
of the migrant Mexicans, in the sorcery
called thirst. Inside train cars. Doubled up
behind the axle of an Oldsmobile—asking
for washer wax, asking for allowance,
straw for night soil. We'll talk
about your asylum hostels in Brandenburg,
Malchow, and Hoyerswerda. Doom's larvae.
Pesticide shacks prismatic, in Parlier, Visalia,
and Kingsburg, California.
A German restaurant there whispers:
What is the path of the Mexican ovens in the bakeries?
We play this music; listen to the horns.
In what forms? you say.

In the dance of chains and broken noses
—Störkraft, Noie Wert,
the KKK Junior League, Brutality Brittanika,
we all rock to the national beat
of Major Hurt.
Music?
My Americanness.
Your East-Westness.
"Metaphysical leprosy."
You laugh. An archaic term.
Xenophobia, you say.
My East-Westness, your Americanness.
We will despise this and then we'll stall.
Point to the human sidewalks; their blue thinness,
Gastarbeiter in their hunched worker overalls
stagger down the avenues. On their migrant hands.
Mention Poland.
Never been there, none of us have.
Poland and Rózevicz (led to slaughter, at twenty-four, he
survived, yes).
We begin to speak of him here;
down the alley. Egg diners
on Saturday mornings, over toast,
hash browns, and juice.
Rózevicz and cigarettes,
Berlin and chocolates.
After we read his poems
we scribble a frenzy. On small wedge-tables.
Our musician friends lean over,
whisper into their lovers' ears,
their long hair over their eyes.
My musician friends use the term emptiness too.
They equate emptiness with fullness. They rejoiced when you
struck the Wall; the gray-speckled sex.

Sledgehammer music
across the mad seas.
My musician friends (students too)
—they play hard saxophones.
Rhythms of chalk dust,
spray cans; an old Mexican record
that resembles the smuggled Russian
Gypsy songs
—when Stalin was alive.
My pale, sallow-skinned
musician friends. Short coats or none at all
wander off.
We roam here. This is accurate,
yes, I think it is.
Video streams, bamboo.
A satellite system of delicate intimacies.
I know this much: Up there
—a giant mirror in the sky.
Mute flurries; in our own trueness.
In fashion malls underground. Without
the telescopic leash at times, Los Angeles
for example (the embers still burn).
We resolve ourselves.
Night nourishments, connecting to the wild,
we step,
to the possum detectives.
Scratch the pregnant bark, blare out its rap song.
Concentric. Halo-blood from tree stumps,
from their hearts. Next to the homeless one-eyeds.
Step to the local plazas, empty and shiny
after the rain. Cellophane,
stripped and naughty under our bare feet.
Presidential news stuck to our big toes.
Students of Berlin

are you hungry, as I am?
Are you hungrier, yes, you must be hungrier.
My wife, Maga, turns away from these discussions.
My wife. A seven-inch scar sewn across her belly.
An intruder wanted her. I search for him.
Day in day out.
I trace his knotted vernacular.
Every kiss slides down the rose thorns.
She reads Zagajewski.
She stares at Frida Kahlo. Flaring headlights
on the bedroom curtains.
She strokes her long black hair. It is black,
so black.
I fall into her arms. I yearn for comrades, I tell her.
But, you're an orphan, you
wouldn't know what brothers are. You
wouldn't know. She says, stroking her darkness.
We stop.
Gaze across the library, at an honorable bird
on the tightwire of the window ledge.
The bird is miniscule,
a blue jack, wet and steady.
Little cosmic engines on silvery animal tracks,
sniffing out our lives behind the glass.
Measuring us for rain, for bread.
Big sky, up—it is frayed, riddled
in blood-bath gardenias.
It is a falling sky. Falling to its own grave,
but where is the grave for skies? In Bosnia they know
about the sky grave. In Los Angeles (the embers).
There are blasts everywhere. I'd like to say
that this awakens us.
As I speak I want
to slither out of my mouth cavity.

I want to write of love
in the face of disaster.
When I eat
my favorite powdered sweet cakes,
the reptile pokes me in the ribs,
a sexual deepness in its eyes;
large crimson, loose.
But then I slump through the short
arduous light of the theaters, the palisades.
I'd like to say I am walking with a little girl
still in my irises. Who do you walk with?
Yes, who do you walk with? Who
still resides in your eyes?
Do you follow her songs?
Into the tilted factories, the smeared taxis,
the stunted universities, into the parlor of bank notes,
in the cramped cookhouse where the dark-skinned
humans still stoop and pitch the daily lettuce bags,
the daily radish box,
our daily buckets of fruit meats? A half-cup of red sausage? Is it so?
I fall back,
I sleep more than I should, I lie down
by the wrinkled sidewalk, draw chalk circles;
meet the hunger artists.
You know them.
They paint their cheeks with crazy eights.
Their sex is full grown, sprawled open.
Their enlarged livers
push out of the thorax, they push out
in a modern shape, the Autobahn, for example.
They speak of fluorescence,
a colossal fixture. Raised hands and necks;
artificial light, over our dark stores,
weary with revolutionary ambitions.

Maybe we'll slip into your new century,
—under your new country—
fondle its embossed fuses.
Tree rot and sperm,
breast milk, tears, spit, and cement fodder,
bullet-sized droppings from above.
We gravitate toward you, the spirit here, inside gravitates.
Well-pressed university shirts; anarchic spiders with bow ties
and briefcases. We weave
an unparalleled labyrinth.
We slide downwards, into the Southern streets.
Barefoot, we arch and kiss,
we exchange notes on the soft ends of the earth,
on the military parade; eerie screens.
Velcro jackets pulling skin
off and on, off and on.
We listen with excited ears, mechanical and fantastic
—with a jealous lover's heat. Our blue greenness speaks in
low scales.

We lean to the cloud and water music;
all night fancies, when clouds lie over clouds
and shape deep thighs over our houses.
These are our charms. The maps we follow.
This is how our brown face is cultured, in this scale, full of
sky shards, ancient, blistering, alone
with each other. Old light
and new light.

THE ROOTS OF A THOUSAND EMBRACES
Dialogues

| 1994 |

I   Mobius

Maybe, here, the body

or appreciation is in the degrees of light, non-line and
texture, especially when the light shaft becomes obscure,
half-lit—when it goes into the sutures behind the gesso of
the cast.

There is no top, no bottom—and of course, no beginning
or end, since the body leads into the other—a mobius
body with one side only and a backside we will never
see, logically; there are only beginnings.

I will repeat all this often. There are no frames,
really.
It goes against the nation of love.

IV   Jade Mother Goddess

Frida came back and kicked away the features.
There was a crisis.

There was a mid-point of no return:
a reddish ovum with tidal waves turning and leaping
beyond its plasma, a jade mother goddess with cactus
shoulders and a puzzled clay-like background broken,
moving around the granite complexion of the moon;
there was a maguey thorn breast, succulent, shedding a
tear-shaped milk drop, and in the center, in one of the
centers, there was a scarlet woman with her black hair
falling down into the roots of a thousand embraces. She
reached it alone. And language (Master-made language)
faltered for a moment, fell apart—yet the Master keeps
on, somehow.

Pretending to speak; writing with the idea that his words
connect with a larger universal system of Master-
meanings. The small invention is simple—this sweaty
speakerly Master.

IX   Tropical Parrots

For us

there are no Macro-worlds. No footing where we can re-
adjust our language and our shape. No enjambments for
our signification. No ready-made molds for our migrant-
shard body, breath. We do not wait to build our
muscularity, our rebel tendon world. Too many have
tried and failed; an old reflex taken from the Master's
theater.

We accept our small numeral, our tiny half-face, our
shriveled embryos—this is why what is in vogue does not
attract us, this is why what is on sale at the Master's
bazaar would be an ill fitting. The Modern-word died at
the hands of a few silver tie surgeons; rugged and
refined ventriloquists of conquest.

Here, in the tundra—there is chalk dust, tropical parrots—
a screaming metro ambulance, maybe, a city with a
woman in the shape of a thorn by a lake that waited for
an eagle to descend long ago.

XII   Style, Genre & Craft

To call

the making of the body-cast a *style*, is erroneous—this
implies loyalty to the Master-sculptor. To say *genre* is
false—this implies residence in the Master-house, to say
craft is evil, even though evil does not exist.

Only the Master-writer knows *style, genre and craft*; the
bearing out, bit by bit (through hard, devoted labor and
academy), of the final literary machinations that directs,
influences, guides and sweeps an entire macro-globe of
orientations, moods, fantasy and interests of Master-
power.

XIX The Game of Color

I am not tragically colored.
—*Zora Neale Hurston*

In the Master-Palace,

especially in the Master-bedroom, there is a palate of
cosmetics for the raped serf. The regime attached to this
scene is called the Game of Color.

Now, I know it is a game. I repeat, now. Up to this point
there has been no clear proof, or better yet, no erudite
concept (a complete concept without the frayed edges of
desperation) that clarifies the intensities of color.

Again: for us, color has always been cast with the notions
of 'darkening.'
On the other hand, for the Master, color has always been
linked to the ideas of 'shining.'

XXVIII   The Barber Sculptor

Frida sports a hummingbird necklace

today, the hummingbird that was caged for so
long for wearing a personal rainbow on her breast; there
is a Chinese screen going up in flames above Frida's
braided hair, and the combed arm of the monkey caresses
her chin, pursing his lips in the fashion of an accountant
who has arrived at the precise figure. The wide-angled
ferns await the next torrent of waters, yet, deep inside
their webbed veins there is a passionate rhythm
beginning to fall in tiny lilac flakes—it is all going up,
straight up from the golden arcs of the solitary chair
where Frida, the raging barber-sculptor, sits quietly with
a clean pair of scissors, staring across the marbled room,
smallish, to the figure of a man, unkempt, proud with his
usual hat hovering over her tilted body, tilted by his
knife and yet, she wears one dancing ballerina shoe.

XXXVII   The Mirror in the Canopy

There is something else to remember:
the mirror in the canopy does not exist.

The Master-game lacks ecstasy. Lacks the piano-like steps
that ascend into the soul of the sea anemone, the
tremulous valley where a crystalline alphabet unwinds
its translucent wisdom—a note, a dance, lit with moon
bits of gold. Here is something to keep in mind—the
thousand dreams in a grain of sand. And what is more—
the eerie calling of the sand in our own waking hours at
the office, at the Market Palace where Frida, the bride-to-
be, takes a number on a wire and the groom-to-be walks
out with a bundle of arsenic, jams it into his glove
compartment and later ponders on the time-dial
wrapped around his thorax, he ponders—on the absences
kicking out from his thin skin, he works on this, alone,
maybe with the radio on, he considers all this again.

LOVE AFTER THE RIOTS

| 1996 |

7:30 pm/Thursday

Below the helicopter, running from the system.
Leaving L.A. Going with these whipping blades,
pulling over my face. They swarm into me,

bellow. In the name of Dante Alighieri;
follow his equestrian milk to the tenth ring,
ragged ivory.

Riot buildings held in orgasm,
circular wrestling, efficiencies
with our thighs that splash

waters of cinnamon guns;
this thief's oboe.

This new world
mechanical bedroom in the center of Ave. X
—outside, yes, there is
chalk dust & eighteen-wheelers on fire.

8:00 pm

M&M
wears the green shirt of the golden Che.
She calls the head waiter at Porky's on Whittier.
We leave, we drink & trade notes
in the basilica.

Sweet serum in the gutters,
licorice transfusions.

We dance Balinese hulas,
swift gold and stiff masks of musk.

Out in the corridors, by the traffic ribbons
night youth still swagger & sell
their love dipped in Michelangelo's hair.

She digs into me.
Nervous snails
on her belly button,
my tropical tongue.

9:20 pm

Back up. Marga talks.
I drive against my best intentions.
Santa Monica, Venice—Albert King on the box.

By the sea & the vices of families
gone asleep in the smoke. 5000 lire
and she does not look at my face.

She says I look like Gregory Peck. The auto
swerves up the alley. She lives alone, now.

Stop for coffee. Read the *Times Mirror*.
Her skirt, my pants. The wheel stays
alone in the night shade. Silence,
a stone, tiny in her boot heel.

12:01 am

Marga is here now,
in furs and blondish beeps.
Her cape turns back into the car.
A wry kiss again to the tiny public.

We are ready to emerge. Is this city
ready to breathe—in flames?
I am swollen with glassy air.

How is this possible? Who are the stars
of the production underway?
Spike Lee's film journal ruffles
in the back seat.

Call me Pinal; I tell her
this was a long time ago.

2:11 am

At the tiny restaurant:
> *Fiore Escavatrice*

Antipasto.
We are always together,
she says. Antipasto—this
is how we begin our conversations.

Pinal, she says, with her wide
and perfect smile, her Mexican elegance.

We talk about our fathers.
A jagged tree appears outside.
Stings me.

3:03 am

The TR-3 spins at 75 kilometers.
Florence Street, an egg. Eat, she says.

Photographers?
Yes, only for you, she says.
Eat it, she says in Italian.

We go by the country,
a miracle is in the making.
People are running.

Where are the children? A scoop
about the raped women in Bosnia.
Their elongated scarves are the clues,
Marga whispers into my tiny ear.

3:07 am

Seven black children are being held hostage
by the vested cops. A Korean, an Arab, a Mexican with a broom.
Bicycles and an umbrella with an old woman.
Upside down, she struggles for her face.

No one can go home now. America,
America.

A grandfather man comes out of the building.
That's it, the reporter shouts
and sings Ave Maria.

3:45 am

She asks them, what are you doing
to put the fires out?
I know she is asking me.

Praying too.

She says
something like this:
A torch, a line of torches, men
in plumber uniforms, in laundry jackets,

a blackened sky with a little boy & girl rustling
their feet in the silk. A vigil. Floating pillows,
crushed bedposts, open night-cream jars.

4:21 am

Just love yourself, she says.
Strum your Indian lute, don't argue about me.
Other words:

mysterious,
maternal,
original,
tiger. These are not the words.

Something about you & me &
this shattered basilica.

Body? Soul? Permit me, this is Pinal.
This is loss, the reporter says,
something that can't make love.

4:48 am

I've read this poetry before. Unlike me.
A living, clear, honest style with subterfuge.

It may happen tomorrow. To live intensely,
in spiritual fulfillment. Marga almost falls
back when I get to fulfillment
on the way to miracle.

Fire drenched
with voices of fire. An American just
walked in and talks about masculine uncertainty,

about quality. What all Americans ponder
in the time of destruction.
Something more stimulating than jazz, he says.

5:30 am

We've nothing to do. Even with the wars,
even with the mobius strip of bodies
tied to me and you, we've nothing to do.
Bring your friend, Sylvia. Bring her lover, Lo.
Bring yourself, Marga. Jump into
the Triumph with spoke rims,
let's get best suckers & meet the reporter.

Meet the naked flames dressed as lovers
in one-hundred-and-eighteen thousand characters.
More drinks to quench the trenches, the glitter
of the military caps and tilted blouses.

6:01 am

Write to me. Marga.
The black taxi leaves plainly.
Two men fight the way men fight when
they are clumsy and wonderful. Cowards.
Next car.

I can go to bed now. My brother is away.
I mumble another place, buildings with ragged windows.
Collared shirts, a little boy with a burning cane,
a painting of Hollywood in the forties.
A sports car with fog lights, the wet streets.

BORDER-CROSSER
WITH A LAMBORGHINI DREAM

| 1999 |

Angel Wrestler (with blond wig)

for Rigoberto Gonzalez

They come & offer maize,
oat gruel.

Blue-red rooster feathers in a ceramic bowl. Cigarettes, wide mouth.
Incense, bowls. Zircon stones, at times, little see-through rice-paper letters
with diamond shapes, names & sonnets. I hate sonnets. Sestinas are for
pigs. What am I doing up here, next to the Nixon posters? No one listens
to me. My back is about to give, my hands are charred from holding these
yellow candles & chocolate coin nets. The wig is embarrassing. I tell them,
go fishing. Come on, get off your rumps, go fishing, throw a line, tear a loaf
of French into pieces, it's the best bait, you know, dump it into the waves,
hurry, go—*nada*. They kneel for a few seconds, adjust their privates in front
of me, they fondle the chair cushion, the velvet one with '60s embroidery.
Inventory time baby, I yell. Count your cells time! Here's a dream with your
mother's head cut off. What more do you want? It's no use, they don't listen.
The D is missing from your DNA! I sing. Actually my baritone voice is fluid,
prismatic & quite cheeky.

Nada.
They sit there, next to my left wing, scratch the bald spots, trace the welts, dig
reddish splotches behind the feeble ear. My back, I tell you, is about to go.
All I have to honor is my face, the nose is still good, Andalusian, my
wondrous breasts. Listen, I take off my Jim Morrison leather boots &
sprinkle confectionary sugar powder on the soles of my feet. Maybe, I'll leave
a couple of footprints in front of their fishbowl, next to the computer office
door. Just me & the collie, the one they leave behind for the Mercedes. We
fly over the sofa a hundred times, crash against the CD collections stacked like
Byzantine churches. Shhh. Mother goldfish is awake. Her infinite mouth
calls me with fiery halos. The eyes play an aqua minuet with devotion, a tiny
tongue floats out of a cloud, a slow explosion goes into white patches, then
rain, the serenity of black mountains, in strange motion, an infinite tear.

Simple Poet Constructs Hunger

Give me Bulgaria,
its demolitions, its contempt for Communism, its pâté of thick-backed
administrators grasping at the old regime.
My nose? You ask. The State has eaten it.

In an apartment
overlooking Dorogomilovsky Market, a homecoming parade
celebrates my return. Three Russian teenagers snap a photo of my face.
A Polaroid in muted tones, a shy type with scarves, then they sit
on a couch at the cafe & stare at a fancy car melting
into the afternoon haze.
One of the boys deserted his military unit in Chechnya. They too are
      hungry;
I can tell by their stiff fingers. The war is over, one says.
Forgiveness or bread?
Punishment or wine? Five thousand march in the iciness, in the ruins.
Searching for my nose with the others, one looks for an ear.

No one notices; Gogol, my dog, leads the way.
Hepatitis & mystery float in the currents of the Aral sea.
Pesticides from the cotton & fishing industries, they say, as the girl
belly bloats with unspoken & hushed desires. Rifle butts
with my ass against a car. Under broken floors.

My clairvoyance fails me.
The spirit drops into a washerwoman's bucket, limp,
weary—the smell of oil & potatoes.

Young Kuramoto

He was a sad angel, Kuramoto—a family man of eight, on welfare subsidies, cheese lines & turkey day festivities, on the welfare benefits of his new nation, a man about town, with a belly & a knack for jokes & tales from the old country, as a matter of fact he had a way of speaking about the old country, Suffering—he would call it, out loud, recalling his intimate relations in that faraway place, he even went as far as meticulously describing his cubed & boxed luggage, how he hauled it from the shores, all this he would recount as he entertained his close associates over a small, thick glass of Anise Del Mono from his village, he played seven-card-no-peek, his favorite, his face would flush, then in a quick change of mood he would jump to the iron belly stove & fry quesadillas stuffed with squash flowers— *flores de calabaza*—another remnant from the old territories. Kuramoto, as you can see, was a man with a fond heart full of sunlit pictures, a time gone.

I've changed my name, he sang one day to his wife, they told me it means Warrior of the Seven Virtues & as sure as you can toss & swallow the sweet syrup of anise, he whispers them, one by one, all seven: kindness, compassion, patience, sacrifice, solitude, contemplation, emptiness, of course, he could not name them all at once, that in itself was a sin. He could not admonish his weary-eyed employers, that in itself a trespass, he could not warn or preach to the local squad of tiny-evil doers, another illusion. It would cost him in the end; Kuramoto was at a standstill, his game was an odd net of solitaire—pull against your own hard-won forces, caress your own trials, smother out the tiny tendrils of your own slippage. From time to time speak to your children & your lover, mention the suffering place, this Kuramoto can do, a permissible move.

Lord Jim

They never found her.
It was her lot. Rómulo said
nobody beats her at Pyramid Palms Realty International.

Nobody messes with her on her own turf.
Carmen'souttheresomewhereIdon'tcare. The husband had a bad habit
running his words together when he was at a loss. This wasn't the first time.
Or the second. Out there. She was. True.

In any case, there was a wrought iron gate (this is central to the story).
The fact remains that the dog, that is, the Chihuahua, known for its Aztec
ancestry, its large parietal bone structure & its unassumingly quick attack
due to its own predestined fate regarding intimacy & human disintegration,
had a number of telltale signs: red spots, dark
cinnamon reddish, detectives say.

She was on the way, they say. Maybe, Finocchio's—
hangout for all nighthawks in Tillamook County;
you could find her clientele there usually sipping a gin gimlet.
Finocchio's? Not a chance.

I've got the report.
Last seen at Lord Jim's—
the quintessential late night spot for tawdry pre-divorce annunciations.
Being a real estate broker, a poet of sorts (she always
carried a book by Anaïs Nin, with journals & neon-colored
crayons, of course), she was a master—
engaging the opponent in arguments about faith, trust & whether
or not she should renounce all her belongings, the job-job
& immediately enlist at the local Zen center.

Highly unlikely,
Rómulo, her sporty husband's lawyer, told me.
In another realm: grass covers her eyes.
She picks away at the earth.

Out. Going out she was.

Someone found a pair of bifocals left at the restaurant.

Witness #1 says:

"Carrera, two-tone wash, gray, with green stripe frames."

NotunlikeCarmentoleaveme. Rómulo.

He knew the husband. Carmen. She knew. Both did.

Five Directions to My House

1. Go back to the grain yellow hills where the broken speak of elegance
2. Walk up to the canvas door, the short bed stretched against the clouds
3. Beneath the earth, an ant writes with the grace of a governor
4. Blow, blow Red Tail Hawk, your hidden sleeve—your desert secrets
5. You are there, almost, without a name, without a body, go now
6. I said five, said five like a guitar says six.

I Found Myself in the Studio of a Tabla Master

for Genny Lim & Anita Leal-Idrogo

In Varanasi, the spirit waters of the Ganges burn death at my feet,
bones, rags, ancient pyres, the first fleck of namelessness, the bodies
go up in singular smoke, in greenish ribbons, a woman at my right,
her left leg bent in the pose of fulfillment, as if about to dance or step
into birth, or dawn, a faded tiger skin at her hips, the Ganges takes her,
healers let go of the child body, with the eyes complete in mute light
the villagers wash, again, lift water to their faces, five counts, five chants,
may Vajrapani return as the last sage, may we learn from the Ruru deer,
her melodious voice for the hunter, the one who arrows only himself,
sing out to Mila, who drank nettle soup for years, until his arms, gaunt
face were as the plant in his meals, the flavor of stillness, a sitar
divides the smoke & jeers, a skull bowl, a curved knife in the wave
dance among the lotuses, a reddish conch shell opens, it is an ear,
my breast, my hand, a forgotten & abandoned scarf that bellows,
the tabla is before me, in my honor they are saying, the players drum
mountain shapes, the child goes down below the horizon, the tiny hiss
flute & serpent leads, charred leaves, my lives into lines on the waters.

We Are All Saying the Same Thing

after Szymborska

Yeti come down. The escape is over—the earthquake
mixes the leaves into an exotic pattern.

You slide down the precipice & spit.
You chew on a Tibetan prayer wheel.

This is our city with the bridge in flames, call it Desire.
This is our mountain, hear its umber harness shiver, call it Time.

& this old woman beating a bluish rag
with her shredded hands—call her now,

call her with your honey-like voices.
She is the sky you were after, that immeasurable breath
in every one of us.

We are all saying the same thing, Yeti.
We lift our breast & speak of fire, then ice.

We press into our little knotted wombs,
wonder about our ends, then, our beginnings.

LOTERÍA CARDS AND FORTUNE POEMS
A Book of Lives

| 1999 |

La Lotería

In my sleep, in this hurricane fiasco
she comes to me. She points to my obligations,
this hammered and merciless Lotto that powers
down from the heavens. Lotería, she whispers.

The triple-horn brother, the one in charge of cement,
birth and peace in the villages—he escapes.
She is not an angel. Or Hera, Llorona, Underground—
Runner. Her foot on my liver. Yes. Her eyes. Yes.
It is her eyes that I fear. The multiplying
numbers of my life gone astray, falling. Levitate,
she whispers, take your cards and explode,
be the kitty-poet who sniffs fortune in the fields.
Be the city face that points toward the ambush
without remorse or regret, with relish.

La Palma

In my last love letter—you know,
well, I gave you everything, nothing
was left untouched—my deepest secrets,
if only I could repeat them once more,
I opened up my shirt, this rivet board
you called my Manhood. In one crazed second
I threw it all away & knelt at your feet
by the shore, the ocean pulled me back.
I wanted to walk with you and for once
see you as you see me, touch you as you
touch me, I was ready to listen by your side.
Our shadows would melt into the other,
they would die and a new form would float
along the wind-sands, two as one, and one
as two, a different two would flower,
the enigma pouring down from the sky
would unravel, the blueness of the waters
also, would break into ice, glass, lines
on my hands, everything I had known
disappearing before me, yes, it was me
without you.

El Fruto

The apple wasn't our true origin.
The tree, well, it offered its own brand of shade.
The parrot you can see him? The witness of this account.
We had just come back from the Serpent Café, rebellious.
We had just washed in black light & oyster sauce.
Our fragrance was of sex, lemon rind and coral.
He mentioned the brutalities of the heavens.
I pointed to the blistered boulevards, the musicians
in stoic delight, their gaping violin wounds.
He mentioned the ecstasy beneath his blonde ribs.
I turned away, called my sisters, Tara, Queen of Illusion,
Mayahuel, Goddess of Dark Jazz Nectars. Then
a delicate voice flashed from above, it ripped away
the milk from my lips, the wine from his eyes.
It was King Executive, Demi-god of the New Business.

El Vuelo

Close your eyes, now—we go,
we slouch toward the city of forgiveness,
we ride, we cloud-rumble, we sigh
the First Sign,

ending—with our hands inside the marble,
the aqueous populations, continents without form,
we slip, we dissolve as we glide, my child
above me, my last loose incantation, to my right
this love streaking from all the faces, other
forms, other lisping deaths, we cry, we whimper,
we stun the extensions of the Void, we forget
where we are headed, it does not matter,

we arrive at the center, we pass each other
without an earth, or sun or galaxy, we burn,
we open our mouths, the first mouths, first
naked without signs, our inner shape is outside
the bluish spark & the black mix,

a dotted bliss
to a silvery hand ahead,
the feminine dome.

El Maíz

I am the speaker
the wild oval sister
of the five mystic colors—yellow,
red, white, blue and the black-violet.

For centuries
they nurtured me, they opened their veins,
frothed their groins and breasts, in a hive
strapped to their back, they kept me in heat,
away from the serpent's wrath; there was ice
and wind. They shriveled from the famines,
wars and the lava in dung heaps.

They left me their tears as nectar, embossed
inside conch shells. On the whittled hook points
of howler-monkey spears they balanced
their memory-pictures. They caressed me,
that is all I know. In ragged muslin dresses,
they laid their plumed shields down
and knelt before me, my tiny white fetus eyes
multiplied. For all this, I will feed you
my body, my warring brothers, I told them,

I will paint your skin as my last aperture
and voice your bones in my infinity light.

El Fuego

I've prayed to her so many times.
To heal my gibberish heart, to bleed my lush liver,
to wash my tiny hands in turquoise nothingness.
I have captured too many beings & held them
too close to my own: this is the illusion.

Now, she kneels before me. In her gallant
conchero dress, her obsidian-center face.
Mexico, her servants shout as they peer
at my thin legs, at my table of hollow domes.

This is not Mexico, I scream back. I am dying
of love, that is all. My own wings drop, sprinkled
with poisonous solutions, with an always-war.
The fire-mouth continuum, the soul-chromatics,
the endless tracks of intoxication; my true
form blows out of her belly. My true night.

El Ferrocarril

After the revolution, we waited by the Ceiba tree,
our old goddess. We were faithful, even under the new rule.
We ate small portions of rutabaga, of piñon nut.
Some strummed their days, others wore dark scarves,
the trees themselves wore dark scarves, almost flames.
I stood gently by them. I noticed the machine smoke
from the West. I noticed the dog with the rabbit face.
I smiled with a new sickness. We all waited. Our bones
shifted into a quiet rebellion as we roared toward
the mountains of the south in despair.

La Serpiente

No one's got me right. That's all I can tell you.
They read the letters of the dead. Nada. They
shut down with their thumbs in their hearts. Here
I call them, here, baby, aquí. I am the Mistress Coil
Obsidian, phosphor and the eye of the murdered babies
in the reefs. They come at me, they accuse me
in the form of silly dagger-mouths. They shout Sinner-
Girl in black and silver hipster hot-pants. They keep
on coming, they got Kaos problems, they got a speck
of Poland under the harsh fuse of a detective's bone.
I burn every point on my skin. I sing uncanny
Spiritual Arias coming up from my last galaxy.
They forget how I laugh. I laugh with perfection.

El Diablo

Fear was expected to wash down the rivers,
the clergy said. Just a couple of problems
fix-it things—the child aberrations, for example.
Farmers kept on with wheat, lettuce, grapes,
the paradox of irrigation. Who tended the flowers?
The war? Well, who wants to answer that? Me?
You? So, it grew up, on its own, this brooding
orphan in our garden.

La Víctima

Don't believe anything I've said. Everything—
I take it all back. It was a sham. The story
about how the eagle forged the sign of a new nation,
the one about the dove, crucified while in
office, the other one about the Healing Vine
that will rain its aroma on all, how it will save
at every step, in every small town and metropolis,
the story of my own birth, how I arrived, without
a father or mother, that I was a boulevard orphan,
that I became accustomed to wild and supple kisses,
the night itself, how it haunts me with its child-locks,
my own nakedness, how no one notices, how
I pull out the spirit-skins from what I hear,
how I lean to one side and disappear into the haze.

La Canoa

for Joaquín Ramón

It is late, it is time to leave. To let go
of the shame-bodies. To forget, most of all.
I've been waiting for you. Behind the masks.
Behind the sideshow, the national awards.
Names, too many to remember. One remains.
Your name. It has no true shape. It has
no rhyme or even letters. It lies here,
in these quiet waters, below and above,
inside and at the center of my eyes.
Please do not expect me to tell you.
I am not who I am either. It is time
to leave. It is late.

El Cometa

It is said, when the star of Rumi burns azul
across the municipios and the goatherders slip
out of Janitzio in their butterfly balsa wings,
when the plumed fire-voices instill knowledge
in every web of maize & the maize speaks,
when we are two sitting upon the roof in white
& Chamula, the Indian, with Zapatistas, takes lands
back, captured by our tiger-masters, when this sky
unlinks and time waves its numerals without wars,
when this house we own dissolves again, a river
will appear, then a lake, sexual in its stillness,
all our eyes will explode all the eyes—in praise.

La Rosa

You called my name,

I remember—you painted
my storms after the century burned. You left me.
My days, well, you said, they were lives
without discovery, you used that word—
Discovery. My rouge voices fascinated you,
the unkempt nights in my tresses, all
radiations drawn in between my heart and
your heart. We were Einstein's chalk lines
crossing over stars and wide seas
into timelessness. Yes, the lascivious poisons
of my thorns were necessary, they were the steps
I took to reach my heights. Each kiss,
an ascension. Now the vase stands as a reminder
of your ashes. The house, arranged in perfect
shadows, an illusion too. I flourish with these
new silences & new loves. I use the word *silences*

for sky.

THUNDERWEAVERS / TEJEDORAS DE RAYOS

| 2000 |

Xunka

for the people of Acteal, Chenalhó, Chiapas,
and all the indigenous communties of the Américas

I

Chenalhó—who?
By which roads?
Among whose blood?

So many huipiles on fire,
Torches without end and mother Pascuala
Her small hands, her eyes of lights and
This forest that crashes
Over my breast.

Villages between darkness and fury.
The coffee vanishes, the harvest returns
In tiny girl explosions that no one can see.

| | |

I

¿Chenalhó—quién?
¿Por cuáles caminos?
¿Entre cuál sangre?

Tantos huipiles en llamas,
Antorchas sin fin, y mi madre Pascuala,
Sus manos pequeñas, sus ojos de luz y
Este bosque que se derrama
Sobre mi pecho.

Municipios entre la oscuridad y la furia.
El café se desvanece, la cosecha renace
En explosiones niñas que nadie reconoce.

| | |

XI

The beasts fled among the canyons.
Women were left, thrown down, their faces sweet
moss and their hands with elegant fingers, knots,
clouds, in search of that tiny
girl democracy, the one that escapes us in moments
of treason and blood garrisons
through the loose thunder
at the foot of Tzontehuitz Mountain.

| | |

XIV

I want to eat a bit of tortilla
but I cannot find the city
the street does not appear, a shredded rose
catches me off guard, a violin
from a mysterious room
on the road, a candle among the ruins
the high silence on my forehead
I cannot find the milk, the fast
diamond of the poor, I search
for my mother weaving her *huipil* of suns and crosses
but I cannot find the small town
I don't see the meager trail, only this box
of troops and Tzotzil women marching
alongside the road, torn to pieces
I follow, with my hard dress—
today I am twelve years of age.

Pascuala

III

They left me, half-buried, among the fields of coffee
full of smoke and leaves and mud and blood. I asked for mercy
with my open arms, but they forbade me to speak—
you are too ugly, what do you know, the lieutenant said.

They threw me with the others, young women and the girls
spotted with pus and open sores and flies and infinite wounds
from their black breasts to the sacred mountains of our gods.
They left me, half-buried, among the fields of coffee.

| | |

III

Me dejaron, semienterrada, entre los cafetales
Llena de humo y hojas y lodo y sangre. Pedí misericordia
Con los brazos abiertos, pero me prohibieron hablar;
Estás muy fea, tú qué sabes, dijo el teniente.

Me echaron con las demás, las jóvenes y las niñas
Chorreadas de pus y llagas y moscas y heridas infinitas que van
Desde sus pechos negros hasta los cerros sagrados de nuestros dioses.
Me dejaron, semienterrada, entre los cafetales.

| | |

XI

Your father's guitar
still lies next to the drinking well.
There in its silent scar
the drumbeat of the mountain is born.

The guitar tilts toward my sewing colors,
my cottons. Its strings are sewn
to my loom, waiting for your dark fingers.
The soldiers search for your father, they say,
but they do not know he is made of wool,
earth and song.

| | | |

XI

La guitarra de tu padre
todavía está tirada junto a la noria.
Allí en su cicatriz callada
nace el latido de la montaña.

La guitarra se inclina hacia mis colores,
mis algodones. Sus cuerdas están enhebradas
a mi telar, esperan tus dedos calcinados.
Los soldados buscan a tu padre, dicen,
pero no saben que él es de lana,
tierra y canción.

Maruch

III

A military tank brushes me, but I escape.
Huaraches and a bag, fists and ashes, the moon whirls.

I go along the edges and explosions.
The country thickens with weeping and bodies,
they open as roses.

Xunka, where?
Pascuala, in what cave?
Makalita, are you running ahead on the road?

Will they be at the gathering by the cathedral
in San Cristóbal, on the grass eating papaya?
And you, Pascuala, do you hear me or am I merely talking
to my grandfather Canek, the specter that accompanies me,
the one that pushes me with a *xawaxté*—
this walking stick of black wood.

| | |

VII

Why am I Tzotzil?
Why was I born in this land of so many storms?

I plant corn and yet I reap gunpowder
I plant coffee and yet I reap mad spirits
I plant my house and yet I reap the viscera
of this fallen earth.

Maruch, Maruch!
The sacred girl of Cancuc calls me
between another bottle of sugar water and needles and bandages.

Maruch, Maruch, wake up, you are almost in San Cristóbal.
Your family awaits you.

The architecture seems foreign, I spit without wanting to,
the night transgresses and stalks the day, mothers
run to me and shake me.

Is that you, Matal?
Is that you, Petrona?

A tiny fistful of red corn am I
I travel through an alien chasm
the acid from my forehead scalds me
I am from Chenalhó, that's what I say
and I break.

| | |

VII

¿Por qué soy Tzotzil?
¿Por qué nací en esta tierra de tantas tormentas?

Siembro maíz pero cosecho pólvora
Siembro café pero cosecho ánimas con rabia
Siembro mi casita pero cosecho las entrañas
de esta tierra caída.

¡Maruch, Maruch!
me canta la niña santa de Cancuc
entre otra botella de suero y agujas y vendas.

Maruch, Maruch, despierta, ya estás en San Cristóbal.
Tu familia te espera.

Desconozco la arquitectura, escupo sin querer
la noche se desvela y persigue al día, las madres
corren y me sacuden.

¿Eres tú, Matal?
¿Eres tú, Petrona?

Soy un puñito de maíz rojo
recorro una extraña hendidura
el ácido de mi frente me quema
soy de Chenalhó, así digo
y me quiebro.

| | |

VIII

Rifles and blue stones
loosened eyelashes and red corn nectars
everything rumbles and folds, the butter of blood
with the *chicha*, Sor Juana's cassock
against the bullets and the coffee
my very own hands, they tremble
and disappear and burn and ignite
guitar against *rebozo*
wounds against the afternoon that never ends
Mazariegos's statue, the coffee fields
of rolling darkened eyes
my thighs between the honeycomb flames
and crucified arms, the stars
the poor woman's bread, the jets
between the doves, sacristies and barracks
and the pines that breathe and whistle
furious machetes, explosion
of knives.

| | | |

XII

Pascuala, the graygreen men continue with their parade.
Their gray breasts, their bitter spotted masks—
once they were our children.

We had the same knees.
We had the same plows.
The cornfields grew the same at the foot of our offerings.

Pascuala, you tear off their helmets. You give yourself to their guns,
to their cruelty and their president of delicate armor.

Pascuala, you shred everything from them—except
this infinite movement, this quake of night against night.

Makal

V

I am Makal,
the child woman of Chenalhó.
The willow tree daughter. My arms multiply
in the temple of the wounded. They cover them and lift them
and weave them through my exact branches.

I build a house, a bench, a chair,
a floor where women dance without cruel ornaments
over their breasts, without blisters or scarred temples
where this river of sacrifice opens itself.

This womb is another willow, little moon leaf
branch of green winds and raw combat. It is of drum,
flute cane and day-break corn.

I visit my father Xun at night.
Nurses come to him. Is it my daughter Makal? he asks.
I am Makal, the child woman of the willows.

| | |

V

Soy Makal,
la mujer niña de Chenalhó.
La hija de mimbre. Mis brazos se multiplican
en el pabellón de heridos. Los cubren, los levantan,
los tejen entre mis varas exactas.

Construyo una casa, una banca, una silla,
un piso donde bailan mujeres sin alhajas crueles
sobre su pecho, sin llagas ni sienes profanadas
donde se abre este río de sacrificios.

Este vientre es otro mimbre, hojita de luna
rama de verdes vientos y de ásperas luchas. Es de tambor,
flauta de caña y maíz del alba.

Visito a mi padre Xun en la noche.
Las enfermeras acuden a él. ¿Es mi hija Makal? dice.
Soy Makal, la mujer niña de mimbre.

| | |

XI

Wind from Chenalhó
broken cornfield, weeping bone

and pollen and tiny machines of electric fury.
You lullaby and pull yourself over the women face down
kissing shawls of nothingness and lights of the underworld
your gilded columns, your fortunes and punishments
diagonal between tanks and machine guns, here
you cross through my slips and my swollen breasts and
the fire beneath my woven blouse of red and green
you are the wise one, your flag upon the residences
of cholera and dissolved bones under puddles, stars
shredded in the pits, foreign signs, birds
unknown, and howls on the verge of miracle
you sleep in my hair and awake in my footsteps.

| | | |

XII

It makes me laugh to think
that five years ago I was twelve.

It was yesterday when I began to grow old.
Older than my mother, who still dances barefoot.

Streets are darker and tremble more.
Men no longer have their harp voices,
I only hear their gears, their double meanings.

My ranchito appears and
I laugh, then I cry, I blow out but I don't whistle.
My little dog does not run out, nor does the serious mule.

My child—will you be a beast,
will you be a thorn flower?

I hide beneath the bed of bandages and quinine.
I want to dig an infinite tunnel
to Chenalhó, me and the ants. I laugh,
cry, sweat—caress my hard belly.

| | |

XIII

The soldiers scratch themselves and smoke.
Sons of a sinister uncle, orphans
of the mountains. The Ak-Chamel will take them
in his Coyote disguise. They follow me,
they pinch my skirt.

They squat at the entrance to the Hotel Santa Clara
where the American press arrive.
They scratch, spit blood and comb themselves.

With my net bag of corn and avocados
I cross to the other side of the street.

I am tired. My eyes dark circles.
My hands tremble in the city.
I vomit green and red. I sweat and wait

for the skinny arms of my sister Xunka.
I go hunched, I melt and disappear
in a sundry goods store, it smells
like a plantation perfumed, dried sausages.

GIRAFFE ON FIRE

| 2001 |

Giraffe on Fire

II

Of the sixty-two
viceroys who served in New Spain, three of them
had private Indian mistresses and fourteen of them had mulatto children.
They flayed skin and drank oyster juice.

They burnt corn tribute to Huitzilopochtli
in the name of Yahwe. I raise my arms to them.

Salud, I say. *Salud*. In the center of the table.
I can see their nakedness; this harpoon, I carry, in their accent.
This invention of being.

I must dive deep to find my father now.
In this office there is little to save except the disintegration
that plagues all species. I have learned to play the piano
and the clarinet. This is my new awareness.

I wear a bluish wig. I have learned to kneel
on water, outside where the old women loosen their clothes.
Ocelotl swishes his knife blade. He shows us his teeth.
The Central Valley coughs and fumbles for words.

How to describe this illusion:
in New York, the metros have rusted on their tracks.

Another homicide tells of this. Chiapas lives on bagels and tequila.
They know the history. They know
where to find the President's children.
They read Artaud in braille and rub their genitalia.

A sandwich, a Cezanne to mix things up a bit. Bologna or
ham on rye, garlic butter. More. Duck sauce and raspberry sausages.
Lobster, *ostión*, and *calabaza*. We must eat.

We must crash through our faces
and discover the new opening.

Eat the gold,
chew the strings, digest until we are ribbons,
reddish and jade green. Chinese and Vietnamese.
Cambodian and Hmong villages in tuxedos. Manila
and Northern Luzon where the Ilongot seek the words
for the new revolution.

| | |

14

I have contributed my forty-five days of labor. Blacks for sugar. Browns for
added galley wash. The women stand in awe at our docile faces. My face has
assumed a new air—sexual and transcendent bitterness. My thighs press
against the railings, into grooves and Spanish masters. Syrup from our wombs
grows sharp and distasteful. Who would have thought of such sweetness?

Who would have beheld such whiteness, ivory and rectangular boards
besides our nakedness? In auction. In time, fashioned into the gaunt juice
sacks of the warriors. Forty-five days again, I turn and sing. Forty-five pubis.
Violet cream. Forty-five premature ejaculations in the chasms between
Tiananmen and old Mexico.

I can see, from the balcony. The bulb, each new cleric's fingers, its tectonic
stitches—potato carriers at the rim of the town squares. Smoke up
through the cylinders and then sing the curdled fish slime. Who will pay off
my debt? The belly eye sinks deeper into me. It caresses me with its new
thinking. Tickles my insides. Brittle womb dolls, coiled. Gladiolas under
boiling skin. Blotches from my past, come up from the tips of my breasts,
my eyes and the points of my hidden hair. The vernacular is broken and full
of stolen figures.

I will quote:
Sembla,
Ursa,
Minora,
Querétaro.

We are migrating to Prague, to Kafka's taciturn bedroom where he keeps a tray of wise apples to hurl at his hunched father. This is how to escape, he once told me. You take a tiny shred of gold, finished and grown secretly inside your laboratory. You take it and place it between your front teeth. Then, you stand, looking askance, as they pass by. Whistle to appear lazy. Yawn to appear intelligent. Soon enough you will move your face. The jaw will go back. The God Ocelotl will grant you one wish for having mimicked kindness.

| | | |

16

Who are you? Bending at the jazz kitchen where they play Thelonius. Where they mash green doors on the piano keys. The pauses are significantly eternal. Police with crab suits. A Courbet above the door, framed in docile colors. Rag clouds in graffiti slime. Door is open.

This is all I have; an entrance to the kitchen, a fallow Stradivarius, wet with sputum and uterus. On top: the bridge puckers in Titian ochre. The torso, cut off. Lime water between the legs, tied and invented for the gaze jazz, the be-bop growl of someone standing like me. Congas, mambo skirts, a skull twisted into pleasure. This was our lot. At Tiananmen. Where we stood against the rectangles in green howl. This was our stance. Between a full line of Caruso and a wall of Auschwitz.

Build a guild, they told us. You must lay down the effigy. Gala must descend, she must be burned, they cried. But we held her up. In chalk dust. In a half-eaten dough ball, we carried her across the desert. This was our stance.

I looked for Sarajevo and Kerouac. Velázquez had escaped. We stood there at the tables of the new inquisition. Our ceramic pottery still showed evidence of Moorish influence. They used our bowls to serve soldiers clean water.

Arabs and Jews,
in broken Macehual Aztec.

We stood there with Gala above us. They turned their engines on and mutilated our widows. They turned the engines on and fed us rice gruel. This was our stance, in that significantly short afternoon by the kitchen's tawdry piano keys.

The Consulado stood their ground. They left us no choice. I looked for the Infanta. She was our last hope. Ruffled in sky throat. The music was at our left, it was inside one of the Friars' dining halls. Full of reddish cabinets, strewn hair and cut fingers. I stood alone in front of the mad cylinders, for a second. A little girl in Spanish muslin was sliding into the drilling groove. I wanted to reach out for her. I wanted to pluck another note from the vented and grilled steel.

17

From the mad hills.
In burnt sienna and chopped Harleys.
Radishes in the bowels of the grilled pheasants—parsley and cauliflower.

The bluish knuckles work the maize dough, they work it into the night. Stuffed sausages, prawn sauce. Cacao from the coast, banana and tiny potatoes, shriveled, dried and toasted. Incense rubbed on our thighs, with coriander braids and spearmint on our faces. Wash the belly with the orange heat from the persimmons, twist the sacred rinds at the small mounds spread across the last horizons. Michoacán, Cholula, Yemen.

Spanish bishops and followers of Zumárraga, protector of the moss children, the ones that walk in jazz beats and still bow to Tenochca and Ocelotl. More radish please, cranberry and corn rot for the dawn star.

We gather in a circle and follow the Smoke and the Tepo Drum with our sad ears and our wary hands. The women circle the fire. Shuffle the dust and spit to the left side. The champagne bottle remains in the Friars' domain, the one-eyed Dominicans. I whisper to Kerouac. He shuffles along with the Macehual women. He lays his belly on the map, the shallow mass graves dug out by the Criollos. Vladivostok, he points and shivers. St. Lara play your keys. Stroke our scars. Cling to our skirts, suckle our breasts, beat this last drum. Follow the ink to Portus Acapulco, to Tiananmen where we wait under the grills, in the one-celled housing. Where we sing with beehives and Gospel somnambulant black sugar mill workers. I lay here. I lay with my arms arched across the anthills. They come to me, they speak in Mozart's infantile voice, they crawl into my ears and eat from the stolen honey I carry. They go down to my knees and crawl up to pubis. The black juice beats their triangle mouths. Frida's again, Georgia's. Gertrude's with asphalt wings. Pink powder, a lost boy with a holy wheel. Ezckicl, Joshua.

18

They want to root out the *conversos*, these Jews at my left. The Consulado searches for them. I laugh and kick the dust. I pick strawberry and plantain. No one knows their whereabouts. Like me. You in Freud's short coat, in Sarajevo's sweet rouge scarves. Chucho el Roto drinks his sack of wine. I know everything about the map. The spoiled code hidden in large cheese wheels, woven into secret hummingbird designs spun at the Obraje.

Drink and scrape the clay. Measure your words. Love the insects, note the jaw musculature. Listen to their watery sounds. Split sky, oven streets. A colonial tavern. And yet, who can discover the malady at work? Who can detect our sinew in the bread? Belly hair. That is all. Mustache wash, onyx sucked into the vagina. A cock, shaved and rubbed hot with anise and cinnamon. A tincture of cabernet, this ruby leather drop from the hungry nose. Siwanava, Goddess of Dead Children, I am calling you.

With my manicured black shoes, I draw your designs in the gravel. May the wind from Chiapas read my letters. The Catholic Kings cannot find me.

They cannot pronounce me in this open seascape. I rest my large hands before your dinner table. I place them as soft constructions for your columns. For the angels that caress your oval-shaped ghosts.

| | |

26

My childhood haunts me. It haunts me

with its jagged face rising up from the water, with its Hitler plate, so ready to strike at the mother's round hand. My childhood faces the sea and wants to turn into sand, into the gold from Cibola and Cadáquez. It wants to lay back with its ruby juice opening its tiny valise.

Who can look into its timeless eye? Chucho? The old Tallensi sorcerers? Who can measure the exact diameters inside its hollows, the velvet spiral inside its Carrara? The noose and the apple float above my shoulders. The foreign hips of the figure on the sand elude me.

A Macehual boy listens to Kerouac, he listens to Gala. Catalonia and Rwanda swirl in the waters behind him. He is not in the chambers by the horizon.

My childhood speaks, spellbound, and curls up. No one could own it if they wished. In the colony, my childhood loses its slippers and climbs up a tree, then a watermelon rind. The eye and the hand, in an ivory glow, in the folds of a convex sky and geometric draft of a feather—the eye and the hand follow me wherever I go. The eye is kindness, the hand points down to the inkwell and the champagne, to the Latin root of love. To the fixations of Count Santiago de Calimaya; how he built a residence in New Spain and left my mother sightless.

Engraved, etched, and hardened in the spleen; I search for my childhood. A shrill whistle signals my findings. Above me in a bluish dome, the Count lies dozing, thinking he has me captive. I drink and slobber his name.

| | |

28

The story comes apart near Gala's eyebrows. This is where the plot shreds itself, where the foreign planet dissolves, the one with the face of Jupiter and the sky plagued by half-eyes—bacteria, with a shorn continent; half of Africa or was it half of Chiapas?

The lines of my face match her jugular; we both go up in an odd column, fast and folded. This language is futile, the letters empty themselves of the ink and the ink spills rough circles and mythic shapes. I want to dream into them to find the next line or the next kiss. Alone this time. The Obraje and the Goddess have curled back into the air; the pulp inside the tree form, into the infinite staircase above Cadáquez in California.

If you hold your hand upright. If you spread the muslin mantle over the tabla. If you sit back for a second. If you raise your voice this time there will be a series of black dots in the mirror. Each one contains the ova for the next universe. No one knows how to decipher this today. No one except Zapata, the old Macehual sorcerer, the commoner who lives out his days in the hidden vault below Velázquez's cave. Velázquez told me this was his own secret. He said that he often spoke with Zapata. I am the one who feeds him fresh cut lamb shanks, he told me. Between my paintings, in the middle of sleep, I go to him and lift the small iron lid over his cell. I call out to him as candlelight falls onto his face. I toss the meat to him and to the jaguar on the opposite chamber walled off by bars of Carrara. Zapata says that the mystery of our lives depends on the spatter of dots and glyphs on the jaguar's yellow pelt, he says it depends on the motion of these figures as the Great Omen paces in the wet darkness. Zapata has the face of a woman, Velázquez said. The lips, the tresses.

Beneath Your Skin

A strange sharp whitish black—you whisper to me
something like centimeters continents, the waning night
is smoke, it is a whip that swings in your arms, stone.
No one really re-cognizes you. Your skin, for
example, is a clasp of nuns on fire or earthquakes
ships lamps open covers from a sexual honey,
an invisible (as always) heat. A reddish
summer sheet. Every number on your throat.
Whirlwinds
Velvet
An arrow coming at you
We sweat and we bathe in our mid-flight
Oval hair Everything that will never
be said on the Mount
since it is so evident divine me.

Bajo tu piel

Una extraña blancura negra filosa—me estás murmurando
algo como centímetros continentes—la noche menguante
es humo, es látigo que se columpia en tus brazos, piedra.
Nadie realmente te re-conoce. Tu piel, por
ejemplo, es un ramillete de monjas encendidas o de sismos
barcos lámparas amplios manteles de una miel
sexual, un calor (como siempre es) invisible. Sábana
guinda de verano. Cada número en tu garganta.
Remolinos
Terciopelo
Flecha hacia ti
Sudamos y nos bañamos en medio de nuestro vuelo
Óvalo cabellera Todo lo que nunca
se dirá en el Cerro
por ser la letra tan clara adivíname.

NOTEBOOKS OF A
CHILE VERDE SMUGGLER

| 2002 |

Óyeme, Mamita

Tortilla Flats, where railroad tracks still cut across the street, Bekins storage warehouse and the old Regal Select brewery specters over me in reddish smoke rings, this bawdy corner where Tía Alvina ran her Mexicatessen, La Reina, packing tortas de jamón con queso for the truckers while Cousin Chente and me folded coquitos into sharp hot pink and white packs on a steaming iron griddle. Can still hear Cousin Tito in the back of the Victorian slap congas to a Cal Tjader groove at the Black Hawk. Tío Beto upstairs patient and quiet talks to a fifties thick mike in "El Hi-Fi" room, his makeshift studio, recording a Mexican oldies show for Radio KOFY. It's been a while since we've talked. Óyeme. Must be around half past ten. Time for a merienda with pan dulce, right?

Remember when you told me one night in the early eighties, "I am worried about you, Juanito?" And I turned around from my miniature writing table, second floor Capp Street, apartment #10, and froze? Your voice had a ruffled and serious timbre. Recognized it and looked away from the small amber light above my head. "I see you looking at yourself put letters on paper," you said. All my illusions of being a poet shrank, the wings of the eagle-writer that sees all twittered into the shadow of a sparrow, a wavy blot of cold ink on a yellow legal pad.

New York City Angelic

JOSH, MY SON, SAID

en route to New York City

Josh, my son, said he'd probably show up with champagne and fire poems.
"Fire writing," he said. Can't get over the simult-intensities between fathers
and sons. My mother's intensity to me: mother son: my own father, Felipe,
his quiet fires/11ᵗʰ street w/amputated leg. Blood splash on the floor razor
cutting his toenails—ol' México style deep gash w/diabetes. This is where
he began to die in a mad push toward rebirth: Chihuahua corn farmer
campesino orphan train jumper teen travel kid to El Norte Cheyenne,
Wyoming, & the myth continues in its Ptolemaic ellipse back and forth to
me. In that creative last tiny torrent he began to build.

2x4's
hammers

& 7" nails he began to hammer. Builder campesino at the age of eighty-two.
Shuffler with the right foot draggin', talker, open-cuento style, nonsmoker,
Baptist Mexicano English-speaking coat & hat man, white shirt & long
johns—he began to build. After his last visits to Tijuana whorehouses at the
age of eighty-two. After his last son, Juan Felipe, at the age of sixteen who
wandered. I wondered in silent cathedrals packed in illusion-sins & books
on Zarathustra & Schopenhauer & Nausea at Mission Beach San Diego on
Saturday mornings, on the R bus to Belmont Park, after my inside world
grew thick & golden & wet marooned & caught & knotted & lonesome
urban in the street blind solar boy on his left wing. He began to build:
orphan drinker of goat milk & women honey, seeker in a worn brown suit,
Denver, 1907, a few blocks from the railroad station: now, hitched with my
mother, out of wedlock, illegal w/o papers—naturalized before the world in
1924, with large speckled friendly hands, seed planter, potato fryer, proverb
speaker & cuentosayer & more cuentos about the "bald man, the itching
man, and the runny-nose man"—or when spit turns to ice in Denver. That
figure, that man on the down slope in San Diego, mid-sixties w/the Beatles
on the tube, Ed Sullivan in bluish black & white on the 9" w/one John
Coltrane "Settin' the Pace" album and one Dion album on my sofa—no

record player. He began to build, w/Vietnam smoldering, w/Mexico expanding into Díaz-Ordaz grenadiers in Tlatelolco, expanding from the Romantic moon swoon songs of Pedro Infante & his metal-plated frontal lobe, dead now, gone into another last plane crash, his mariachi suit moist in semen, broken guitars & all the young sharp-haired & hi-toned & prayed-out Mexican boxers dancing in the Tijuana bullring—El Ratón Macías vs. Davie Moore in the rain among thousands, in the mesh-light culture carriage of Catholic devotions. My father w/a busted vessel & torn walker foot bleeding nonstop express to oblivion, destiny—Renada town; he began to build a new leg, a 2x4 campesino leg. Make sure he can continue the flight-spiritual, the flight to my mother w/pains in the belly, w/blood alarmed in her menstruation womb. She caresses a cat over the torn sarape sheet & she looks away as I take her photo gaping hole openness of our tiny apartment, in that place San Diego, in the midst of things, the world dividing, exploding, damaged, sewn back through stone, grass, rocks, capillaries, desert & trains.

Do the meditation:

The father guitar cuento song eternal
The mother no longer sacrificial, yet holy
The son, now walking, always walking
The house, gone up in tribal ashes, gone
South to emptiness
Gone to the earth sky river melody
No chain
No shame
No name.

Undelivered Letters to Víctor

#8

What are we renewing?
From what to what?
How long-suffering is the transition?

The concept is provocative, Vic, archaic, the whole thing about rising
from the ashes, dressed in campesino shorts, working off a molcajete, the
good ol' Indio Chicano stone mortar and pestle, mixing diverse elements,
mashing them into pulp and juice, into a new blood force. Resurrections
without a body, or is the body the words, the dead poesy? Resurrections?
Have we been locked into a religious frame, a vicious and regressive
underlying morality play without knowing it, the grammar of the Second
Coming? And yet things and moments seem pliable, transformative, we
move out into the open mix of coffee houses, homeless tenements, beaten
down chartreuse movimiento rooms, past the old Victoria Restaurant,
Gómez-Peña's loft on César Chávez Boulevard with velvet O.J. Simpson
paintings on walls, New Age gargoyle trilingual lowriders, swamp art
spaces, Kulingtan workshops & Pinay poetics, verse-riffs and performero
doo-wop, mercados featuring papaya and jitomate sales, gentrified Victorians
cutting through the old Irish, Mexicano, and Latino neighborhoods; things
appear new, our poesy missions appear refurbished, then the fog from the
Pacific rolls in again, homicide stats pile up on the curb, more death, then
light, rain, more rain.

I, Citlalli "La Loca" Cienfuegos

SUTRA ON THE ADDITONAL COUNTS OF SUFFERING

Late night:

Don't lissen to him and his rants,
I, Citlalli Cienfuegos burn alone—

What does he know? Knows nothing about my city of green winds and
reddish skirt lust lights over Market, reddish as in the fingers and rough elbows
of the teen Latinas in search of a diamond, let me say it this way, in search of a
kiss from the machine time-keeping unit. I stand alone in the rubble ground of
Tortilla Flats, warehouses of bound bedrooms, fastened tongue prisons, only
worker ants with anteater noses live here, a tropical blast from inside saves us,
at times, saves our sexual wasp-shaped torsos from additional counts of
suffering and loss and emptiness. Lissen to my night, lissen to my dance, my
black feet land on the street pyres of poets and word blower lamps hanging
from their tiny hands, their misshapen podiums. We gather, we frost, we foam
on the corner between rails and concrete, between condos and Plexiglas mini
fashion malls and barber shops colored in Huehuetenango orange stripes
mixed in with lilac. I desire this night, this stone worship night perfect for
thick leaves, storms, and Rio de Janeiro nakedness. My dark cinnamon thighs
feel the night heat, the night beat of crazy fingernails against the hotel brass
beds, the winos sucking in another forty-ounce bottle of prepaid love malt.
Who can count the kisses? Who can measure the slime thousands swiveling in
their tiny cots against oblivion and its agencies of corporate gangster howl?
I count the kisses and the shades that cut across the face in the last breath, the
last gaze of the hospital beds where the old and abandoned shrivel, here in
these sacred streets of blackish jazz talkative gutter shrunken apartment rooms
bejammed into everythingness and void. I, Citlalli Cienfuego, mistress of
illegal flamencos in spasm and orgasm idioms—this is my cabaret. Who can
write it, who can trace its moist pubis?

Undelivered Letters to Víctor

#10

1996 looms over me. I still think of José Antonio Burciaga, whose funeral we celebrated a few days before you went up to New York in early November. At Babaar's, we toasted to Tony—this is for José Antonio, we said as our faces slipped and blurred. He was just coming into his own, you said. After so many years making poetry, since '74 the Centro Cultural de la Gente in San Jose, with his infamous makeshift priest outfit reading "Letanía en Caló" to the crowds, after all the *tertulias* and barbecues he used to have in Menlo Park and his "Drink Cultura" T-shirts, his "Last Supper" murals at Casa Zapata in Stanford and his irascible penchant for political cartoons and acerbic journalism. His new book *Spilling the Beans* had just come out and then blam, just like that, cancer met up with him in a few quick merengue steps. His kindness stands out, it was his kindness, carnal, wasn't it? It was that simple—no rhetoric—kindness. Margarita Luna Robles got it in her to go up to Monterey and visit him on his last days. "Let's make him some enchiladas," she said with enthusiasm. Víctor, you should have seen Tony's face light up. "Just like my mom used to make them, El Paso style," Tony said, then we talked a while, he popped a dozen New Age snake powder pills, Cat's Claw, and we embraced each other. He was tired and lay down next to us. Around midnight, after Margarita and I left Monterey, as we passed through Hollister, two owls appeared over a telephone line. "Did you see that?" I asked Margarita. "He's not going to make it," she said in her typical straightforward voice. "Who is the second owl for?" I asked myself. Who? Who?

The second owl is for all of us. For Mario Savio who died a few days after you received your NBA medal, for his Free Speech time bomb set off decades ago (who will light it now?), for the Pocho-Che Collective and their attempt to create a new poetics—a Che Guevara face with palm tree hair superimposed on a Mission Street mesera, a "Tropicalifornia" and then the cultural centers along with a myriad of raza shops, teatros, and centros and casas that continue to work through the coups and power plays, echoing the power-shamble takeovers that blister through the city-system and the nation at large. The second owl is for the Red Nation writers too and their peyote orange juice vision of magic stone mothers and plumed-jacket fathers, you know what, Víctor, we came close to building Teotihuacán II, "city of the gods," in the tiny farm towns and steely desolation rows. Close, baby. All that is gone now and in some way it stays with us, the way river ringlets keep on expanding into infinity. José Antonio is away now and his funny, political, bilingual, El Paso vibrations, that easy twang of spoken Chicano frontera jive, riffin' on borderlands realities, la migra, el chuko, las locas, el refín, gone too. And they remain as well. All the tasty molcajete raps we've been cooking for the last thirty years, the stuff no one published except ourselves, the stuff no one came to hear except ourselves and a few lefty wanna-be Latinos dissipates and re-emerges. This sounds religious and pious again, a bad Chicano habit.

June Journals 6-5-88

Sunday.

There is an empty Foto-Mat store on 11th Street and San Fernando, next to San Jose State University's favorite laundry, a few feet from a 7/11 shop where most of the abandoned wanderers float from the halfway houses a few blocks away. Shriveled rose petals, cutout notes pasted on the iron grid windows, the best poem in the world taped to the door, laser printed. Here, in this brick cubicle, a young woman was stabbed to death recently trying to make a living by taking foto orders. When I read the poem on my way to teach my prison workshop I knew this was a *poem*. No publisher. No price necessary. No pages numbered. No sales clerk. No one waiting to see the poem or even hear the poem. But, it was the loudest poem, the most magnetic. A swollen tear, a naked vein, a deep green vine with the ability to turn its head in any direction, day or night and scream and breathe and live.

Undelivered Letters to Victor

#9

I want to rock in Tede Matthew's America and his Hula Palace—remember
Tede Matthew's? Tede out-gay talking about Nicaragua, doing the reading
series at Modern Times? Tede working hard through AIDS, through pain
and the end, with gaunt face, febrile fingers, and starry eyes? Tede's drawn
face calls and his clear eyes peer through me. Battles, missions, random
intersections, chaos, time and culture boosters, explosions; I want writing
to contain all this because we contain all this—is this closer to what you
mean by saying we are Americanos? Is this your mission? You know, Víctor,
I am going to say it—no more movements, nothing about lines or
metaphors or even about quality and craft, you know what I mean?

June Journals 6-13-88

Gazing across the table. Margarita Luna has just finished organizing
a Chicano Floricanto literature festival at Stanford University. Marylin M.
taped it on a Nagra. We've been working on a film for quite a while on the
story of Chicano Park, an odd spot of ground underneath a slab of concrete
stretching from the coast of San Diego to Coronado Island where high
school choirs visit ivory hotel lobbies on Christmas; Chicano Park—an
obscure patch of land taken from the gloved hands of the city and the
highway patrol in the early seventies.

Floricanto Literature Conference, a beginning for Chicano poets coming
together on November 14th and 15th in 1973 at USC. Óscar Z. Acosta,
Alurista, Tomás Rivera, Teresa Palomo Acosta, Alejandro Murguía, Omar
Salinas to name a few, mostly men. What really happened? We pulled out
colored scarves, a feverish clown, Goya with tinted spectacles. I sang with
my guitar. We spoke of Amerindia, our new nation gilded with the color of
our skin and with the deep touch of our grandmothers. But no one dared
speak of grandmothers. Chicanas did. Men uttered the priestly psalms of an
Indian Paradiso, now to be reconjured. Except for Z. Acosta. "Put out the
lights. I don't want this to be recorded," he said standing in silhouette.
I was angry. I wanted to see another clown. But he was a clown of darkness.
So he read chapter 14 from *Revolt of the Cockroach People*, his novel in
progress—without light; the story of a vato who is hooked by the cops and
strangled in his cell with the magical tie of arranged suicide. A beginning of
our sound: Goya with and without spectacles. Fabrication and Madness.
Men in line signing books.

June Journals 6-25-88

The check I bounced was for $208. My buddy, Alfonso S., did the design
and layout for Víctor Martínez's first book, *Wrecking Them Back*. I feel like
telling Vic to forget it. Ain't got the dough. Shit. Another good book down
the great tar pit of Chicano scrawl. Now what? I know Víctor has something
cooking in these poems. *Zyzzyva* just published "National Geographic" in
their summer issue. And now, even that micro-crack in the North Americani
Universe of Chicano Chance is over. Víctor has the biggest voice in Califas
at this very second. But it is leashed. Or perhaps it gains fetters when it is
published? I think so. This is the tightrope we walk. Wait for Juan Godot to
publish our stuff or just let him roam, loose-toothed, and angry at readings,
rallies, tables, and sidewalks? What shall it be: North American Literary
Order that is "Craft" or Sabotage, our openness without official gatekeepers,
word gendarmes?

I told Alfonso I would pay him in cash. He said the check was redeposited
by his bank. I wish my bank would do that once in a while.

I, Citlalli "La Loca" Cienfuegos

SUTRA ON THE NOTEBOOK

I stand alone, I hold a thousand lights in my teeth, my throat is sacred, my voice rises on its own, without the charter, only the rebel fuse, the wise elder mothers and my handsome lonely sharp-faced teen sisters, we make a fire circle, we brew the necessary liquids and nectars, topaz, obsidian, and emeraldine, reddish and deep, the caldrons are full, who can decipher us, who can locate our braids, who can truly grasp our undulating hips and fill our hearts with black sweet light, the creation spurt, this song I am singing without names and numbers and myths of time and becoming, I ask you, leaning by the armored street future? Are you ready, are you willing, are you in position or will you walk on by and carry the notebook full of nothing you know or taste or die for? The machine waits for you too, the tubing, the ancestral mezzo mump transformer interpreter translator of your self in birth form. Hear it? Can you detect its sirens? Can you alter its passage through my city, this umbral specter of sleeping moth figures.

I, Citlalli "La Loca" Cienfuegos

You must help me. I can only sing. I can only speak from this golden sea. My feet dance on the mist, my hands high up, open and close, fold and crest with the starry tree, la ceiba sagrada, the universe blanket I carry, you who come, you who ride, you who crawl hunched you hitch your revolutions, you cross from Monrovia and Kosovo, you walk barefoot and laden with sacks of border corn from Tehuantepec, proud and ebullient, long and short voiced, you come to me, here, you from Pristina, you from el Norte, el Sur and you mix into my Chinatown, my Filmore, my Irish stone, my Miwok and Castanoan catechisms, my Sausalito floors, my Sicilian caves of desires and furies and deaths and rebirths, incandescent and gloomy and full of solar change and solar epochs, you embroider yourselves, you paste up your old incense and then in a minute, no, in less than a second, you forget your eternity, your toes touching infinity, you look down at them and you laugh, you take everything, here, everything you can from Tortilla Flats except one thing, yourself, this you leave at the steps of the local machine entrance way, the local mechanic displacer, time stepper, and bender. I have no commandments, no books, no way, no rule, you must touch, but it is not me I am really speaking of, you must swim into another audience tonight, the audience that always speaks back, the one that hums with every leaf and wave and wind, the wind itself, the fire itself, the waters raging in the blue eyelash of the heavens, look up, now, you, look up, it is all unraveling, above and below, there is nowhere to stand, nothing to say, or write or act or be.

Óyeme, Mamita

I AM THAT PAPER

I am that paper, I am those words now, the ink burns pyres in every cell. When I look out to the trees, the long winding streets of Tortilla Flats, as they shoot to the hills and cut the electric rails of the Muni buses to the towers and Twin Peaks, the fog and into the sky haze, I see your signs, I read your voice, now I do. Yes.

Óyeme, Mamita, óyeme—now that you are gone into the deep and silent luminous fallen side of the night. Óyeme.

THE FIVE ELEMENTS

NEW WORK

The way that can be spoken of
is not the constant way . . .
　　　—LAO TZU, *Tao Te Ching*

WOOD

Fisher of Poets

for M. Medrano

His kindness is legendary, his outpourings, who would
sacrifice so many years in the brine, casting nets with jagged maps,
shredded ropes, swollen oars, bloated hooks, barefoot, abandoned,
his hair white, leaves down the rivers, currents under driftwood green,
the stars, yes, the stars, he says, they are the torn eyes of god,
so I must search for poets, except I cannot see what god sees,
so, the fisher finds his purpose in this manner, made of magic
and torture, darkness and laughter, he grasps a willow,
a thistle, a silk-thin eucalyptus reed, this, he says, is her face,
fragments of cloud catch on his hair, this, he says
is her heart, that is all he needs—so he swims back
to release his blue lines with his tiny rough wings
half-washed in crystal light and eyes scorched black-deep

Follow Różewicz

". . . at twenty-four
led to slaughter,"
he recites, smokes his thick cigarettes,
his tenor voice betrays him, his endurance
all these years, he utters so many things
about days gone and villages raped and
winters that lasted decades, how the women
clenched their hands and held their backs
through the storms, the bitter rooms
made of mud and gas, he describes
the pellets, the singed flesh, the water
of ears, mercury and nipples and hair,
he stops for a second or two and dusts
his coat, I hadn't noticed it, the lapels elegant,
pinned with messages, little reeds and stones,
a candle, a vase, a doorknob, a crib and a crutch,
stained letters curled into roses

Note: Tadeusz Różewicz is a Polish post–World War II poet and playwright (1921–).

FIRE

The Trains of Alcalá de Henares

Empty, made of scarves, notions, directions,
calendars, tight dresses and large shoes, maps, a literary
treatise, they were drenched in desire, laughter, sugar water,
diets, hats and fluttering whispers, alone, they were alone
most of all, lifting with the umber lacquer of time and its
opposites, tall, thin, oblique and blue stunted briefcases
reserved with the secret threads of revenge, this
infinite fuse tied to you, please remember, I am speaking
to you—and a scream, if mind and shrapnel could scream
I am not saying this clearly, the trains were bound
toward each other, to the earth and the Spanish seas, their round
arms and jagged watches expanding and exploding our lives

Note: Alcalá de Henares, a historic Spanish city 30 km northeast of the capital, Madrid, was the site of terrorist train bombings on March 11, 2004, where 191 people perished and 1,700 were wounded.

La Plazita

for Ray Gonzalez

Every morning my father walks with the rhyme
his shoes off beat, the hand-sewn patches of the heel
he goes, after the fried potatoes in the black skillet,
when I am wading in a dream, a yellow field without a name,
and my mother is in half-sleep, singing and preparing,
there is a bench and there is a friend there, they
talk and laugh and notice the fountain tell its stories,
this is how every day begins and ends at eighty-two,
the words aren't necessary, when he opens the doors,
he gives my mother an odd roll of paper he found, he tells her
about other days when he walked the same way in
another country, when he talked to other friends
in the same place, maybe Ciudad Juárez, 1956,
the town is small and sometimes when I pass through
you can hear the thousand tongues of the fountain,
birds make an incredible arc, a parabola with centuries,
ciphers and cruelty, experiments, no one sees this, I know,
they are living other lives in another time

Water Water Water Wind Water

for New Orleans and the people of the Gulf Coast

water water water wind water
across the land shape of a torn heart
new orleans waves come louisiana the waves come
alabama wind calls alabama
and the roofs blow across red clouds
inside the divine spiral
there is a voice
inside the voice there is light
water wind fire smoke the bodies float
and rise

kind flames bow down and move across
the skies never seen blackish red bluish bruised
water rises houses fall the child
the elders the mothers underwater
who will live who will rise
the windows fill with the howling
where is the transfusion where is the lamp
who who in the wet night jagged in the oil

waves come the lakes loosen their sultry shape
it is the shape of a lost hand a wing broken
casinos in biloxi become carnations across the sands
and the woman in the wheelchair descends
her last breath a rose in the razor rain
uptown on mansion hill even the million dollar house bows
in the negative shade someone is afloat
a family dissolves the nation disappears
neighborhoods fade across lost streets the police
dressed in newspapers flutter toward nothingness moons
who goes there

under our floors filtered wooden stars
towels and glass gasoline coffins
the skin of trees and jalopy tires fish
bebop dead from the zoo the dogs half drag
ward number nine miss Symphony Spikes and
mrs. Hardy Johnson the new plankton new
algae of the nameless stroll in the dark ask
the next question about kindness
then there is a bus a taxi a hearse a helicopter
a rescue team a tiny tribe of nine year olds
separating the waters the oils and ashes
hear the song of splinters and blood tree sap
machine oil and old jazz trumpeters z's and x's
raffia skirts and jujube hats and a father man
holds the hand of his lover saying take care of the children
let me go now let me stumble stumble nowhere drink this
earth liquor going in petals

stadiums and looters
celebrities cameras cases more water cases
again and again a new land edge emerges
a new people emerges where race and class and death
and life and water and tears and loss
and life and death destruction and life and tears
compassion and loss and a fire stolen bus
rumbles toward you all directions wherever
you are alive still

EARTII

No sé por qué piensas tú
soldado, que te odio yo,
si somos la misma cosa
yo,
tú.

—NICOLÁS GUILLÉN,
Cantos para soldados y sones para turistas, 1937

I don't know why you think, you
soldier, that I hate you,
since we are the same thing,
I,
You.

—NICOLÁS GUILLÉN,
Songs for Soldiers and Beats for Tourists, 1937

The Glue Under

The glue under
and in between the camps and the settlements
attracts me, shames me and leaves me in whimpers.
I want to answer the Glue-Smearers, the Glue-Squeezers,
the Glue-Smoothers, most of all, you read this too, I know.
I shall speak in short rubble letters.

See

        that
        cloud

                It

                                was

                                a house
                                amber lit

                a few
            seconds

                                                  ago

we
were
about

        to
        go
        for
        a walk

      before
      the
      curfew

        hour
        we
        were

                going

to
                          talk
                    about
          our

separation
now

       I cannot
       imagine

                such
                a
                separation

    I
      am
left
in between
separations

                      It
                   was
                   a

         cloud

a
house

           we
           were
           going
           out
           for

        our
        last
        walk
           we

were

going

to

construct

something

in the

coming

months

a proper

end, then

a beginning

Nasser &
Sakiena
This
is
their
story

These
are
not
their
names
they

cannot
be pronounced I am writing on the rubble of the dead—
that is all.

This is not a *lyric* as they say in the Nomenclature.
This is not a *manifesto* as they said in Rodchenko's Moscow, it is
not even a dream or a poem anymore, I want to say,
"This is a table . . ." like Różewicz says. This is a table, this
is not a napkin, even though I shed many tears
entertaining my musician friends at small wedge tables
with slender greenish flasks of cold wines,
our brass-colored faces howling drunk equations
only we could decipher—

this is an elementary school drawing
of apples—in a buried city without borders.

Will You Visit The Rubble Museum

Will you visit
the Rubble Museum soon:

The rubble cobbler's shoppe
The rubble throne (if I can call it that)
The rubble swallower
The rubble begetter
The rubble baker (I am fond of him)
The rubble seamstress (like my mother)
The rubble gardener (like my father)
The rubble wheelchair (I will mention this later)
The rubble mosque
The rubble documents (this is continuous)
The rubble codes and secret rubble jugglers
The rubble suicide jackets
The rubble scarf and coat (they are the same)
The rubble pet rodents
The rubble school in triangular shapes
The rubble toilet
The rubble heart peering through the wound
The rubble theater (in every shawl)
The rubble sack of rubble potatoes
The rubble bed of rubble dreams
The rubble marriage of rubble blessings
The rubble burials—wait
Rubble cannot be buried (its only virtue).

So many rubble prisons
and rubble guards again.

I Am Merely Posing for a Photograph

I am merely posing for a photograph.
Remember, when the Nomenclature
stops you, tell them that—"Sirs, he was posing
for my camera, that is all." . . . yes, that may just work.

My eyes:
clear, hazel like my father's, gaze across the sea, my hands at my side, my
legs spread apart in the wet sands, my pants crumpled, torn, withered, my
shirt in rags, see-through in places, no buttons, what a luxury, buttons, I
laugh a little, my tongue slips and licks itself, almost, I laugh, licks itself
from side to side, the corners of my mouth, if only I could talk like I used
to, giggle under moonlight, to myself, my arms destitute, shrunken, I
hadn't noticed, after so many years sifting through rubble stars, rubble toys,
rubble crosses, after so many decades beseeching rubble breasts—pretend I
came to swim, I am here by accident,

like you.

My face to one side.
Listen to gray-white bells of rubble, the list
goes on—the bones, hearts, puffed intestines,
stoned genitalia, teeth, again I forget how
to piece all this together, scraps, so many scraps,
lines and holes.

The white gray rubble light blinds me,
wait, I just thought—what if this is not visible,
what if all this is not visible.

Listen here, closely:
I am speaking of the amber thighs
still spilling nectar on the dust fleece across Gaza,
the mountains, the spliced wombs across Israel, Syria.

The amber serums cut across all boundaries,
they smell of incense, bread, honey—the color
of my mother's hands, her flesh, the shrapnel is the same color
the propellers churn.

K's Mother Speaks of Her Years in Kuwait

K's mother speaks of her years in Kuwait,
the exodus from Palestine, then the Gulf War,

"We were 400,000,
engineers, scientists, architects . . . true artists
building, creating,
then after the war . . . 30,000 . . ."

I walk before the mirror again:
timelessness, my heart beats against the armor
The-Thing-Against-Itself, the sound is even,
then no sound.
The shit-hole has no walls, dung heaps pile
on the rubble, the nightsoil man sweeps
with kerosene, burns it in the night, wipes his face.

Poster

Listen to me—

gather chalk dust and mortar, notice
that shoe store in fashion, a poster of the Nomenclature in bikini,
hugging a peccary, cone hats and the dialect of a military adviser, the
mustard-colored leotard, stockings and ballerina slippers, rouge and black
velvet curtains, the entertainment, I forget to mention the medals, the
performances, the tickets, sales and pronouncements, video flash, the
editing rooms in prepared shock, make-up for the commentators, the
judge with halibut sauce on the mustache, the bravado, bullrings of sorts,
yes, a bullring with blind philosophical bulls and perfumed bullfighters
in pheasant shapes and crepes on the altars, antiseptic creams and soda
bottles, foam and plastics, fancy corsets, other trappings, incisions, new
folds and enlargements, the ironings, the starched collars, coattails and
the exhaust from the kitchens and satellites, rust in between the fruit,
refrigerators en masse, neon white gills and produce from Sri Lanka,
psychiatrists bent at the waist with giant needles and diplomat pants,
some inserting bulbs and chronometers, on and off switches for dryers
and television screens, the rubbery frames for aquariums, micro-chips and
electronic notices and sardines on Art Deco glass trays from the eighties,

everyone is singing,
everyone is dancing,

excuse me, everyone is slouching on each other, a slow dance,
a melancholy reenactment in an amusement park, a corporate
gala to be sure, it is all so authentic, there is an
executive officer waving a flag and a choir
blowing a small rough harp preparing to sing
a cappella, a Big Legion president arrives, the Ministers
of the Curd and the Onions, also large tubes
of brine water used for the radishes, they arrive too
in limousines, a wedding most likely is taking place,
there are instruments too, tubas and glockenspiels,
marimbas and oboes, a tympani, a Brazilian native

performer from a Xavante lagoon, the treasurer
of one of the clubs arranges the band's musical score,
a fugue in G minor, the group is highly interested
in the Pledge, the wordings, the voicings,
the glassy confetti and drums drown out the tiny ochre bells
in the distance, the small flashes of a rolling blast.

Welcome,
someone says.

Then, the water rushes in, for a moment,
we are still and nude. For a moment, the war paint
and clown designs are enjoyable and brilliant.

I Walk Back Nowhere

I walk back—nowhere,
under moonlight. The dogs look as if
they are angels, the ones I never imagined,
with drooling silvery rays and torn behinds, yes,
glowing in a strange and excited phosphor,

dancing
out of rhythm, racing up trees, chasing
snails. This is like a children's book.

O, yes, the children
with rectangle heads and sack stomachs.
With the eyes of Da Vinci, sad and impish,
meticulous as Ibn Khaldun and taciturn as Nietzsche,
phlegmatic and bitter, when they speak they leave
opalescent liquids on the grasses, stuttered

under a half-erased mural of Arafat, or
is it Sharon,
wait,

the children never speak,
they nod their heads, they carry huge
bundles strapped across their foreheads.
They weep under newspapers and roll up
their skirts and wash them in the gutters,
ponds, if they find them, then they run to the sea.
This is where we meet, on occasion, we

make up stories, we remember fruits and produce
as if blessed by the plutonium blasts.

"Remember the pears, they were so green,
and the avocados, like guitars, honey-golden, and
the asparagus, like a lion's rainy mane, and . . ."

Our mouths water. Their mouths water,
I am used to these stories. I am used to the land
barren, bitten and aflame with lies. I am used to
our faces in this new wild dispassionate light.
I learned this from my musician friends, from
years waging futile wars with poetry until
I could not think of anything else.

METAL

Rejoice dancing on needle.
　　—CHÖGYAM TRUNGPA,
　　　from "Miscellaneous Doha"

Artist Paints a Flower

Dried leaves soaked in gas,
or she holds up the braids of her mother, the ones she's carried
in a ragged handkerchief all these years, she takes a half glass
of alcohol and smoothes it as a brush and the tiny table as a palette,
she has only a few words to paint with, hunger—salt, if only she

had love as one of her words, or a model to sit before her,
to speak of lives gone and coming into being, the painter
wears a dull dress, she sits on her bed when she is finished
drawing the proof, the lines wry, made of icy shadow, crows
across the street, a limp raven dressed in pale obsidian,
the curtains blur with dying light, it is time to rinse
her tresses in the sink—apply color, then ammonia,
the door opens and the vapors wander out into the avenues
of buyers and sellers, and slow figures hunched in traffic,
she takes a piece of bread and paints a piece of bread,
a knife and paints a knife, she takes fire and
paints flowers crashing against the heavens

We Sip Tea and Spoon Gruel

We sip tea and spoon gruel at a restaurant,
it is splashed with bodies and starry earrings,
hands mixed into the potatoes, little noses
under the porridge, metal half-faces, lobes
and upper lips, gnashings, rouged fuse-wires,
switches under skirts and knuckles

a new pulse, the dawn filaments
of sea anemones, the eggs in blood orange chili
sauces, trapezoid dances of bones and plastic
explosives, the forks are no longer forks,
the coffee no longer coffee.

It is a test tube, where we live—
a test-tube colony, maybe the Nomenclature
is interested in the outcomes, I think otherwise.

No one is at the table,
the microscopes are empty,

the radar is on a more tremulous track—
stellar, cosmic, if I may use that word,
cosmic and territorial.

Prepare the future occupations in space—
without bias or cultural tone,
the Nomenclature drives at this objective.

Listen. Listen with your hard ears,
with your Warhol Brillo Box looking as if it is

a Brillo Box
or a Hamburger Jingle
or a Universal Collection of Suffering Songs
as if it has nothing to say, as if it has nothing to shape.

It is non-essence, non-being, non-reading, non-entity.
It operates on its own, it is its own cause, its own
dissemination machines, it provides its own
self-made mitosis, it is a genealogy without origin,

vast,
timeless,
infinite,

plural and non-existent,
wet pubis and abyss,
word and gamma-ray,

a neutrino perched on a string
of no-seeing.

This is why the Nomenclature races into the night.
Ahead of destruction, ahead of creation. Let's put it this way:
Stop asking questions.
Stop resisting the rupture.
Stop grasping the form.

Listen:
recognize the rubble. My mother's rubble sky.

How she carried it on her back.
How she was forced to take it into her belly womb
(a vertical scar of seven inches).

How she wore it
so that the Nomenclature could not decipher it.

Yard Sale in Mid-April

A briefcase
where he stored grandfather's papers, an abacus,
then a fake gold clock with two bells on its head, an odd barbeque
for inside-the-house cooking, about the size of a three-layer cake,
a pencil from Russia with a green tip for sketching, the sky is above
all this, not in a religious sense, it notes this delight I take on rare
occasions, then it continues its own miracles, it does not matter
that I am not seeing things, matter, space, future, spirit,
all this does not matter, I step into the kitchen, give the abacus
to my niece, tell my daughter about my cooking, wander outside
under the clouds.

I Forget the Date

I forget the date:
en route to Austin, Texas: soda on tray.

Women at the computer, mexicanas
learning to read and write at the same time,
a workshop, we exchange stories

the crossings:

Hidalgo
Texas
Sonora
Zacatecas
Chihuahua—I think of my father, for a moment—
I see him again, robust, alone, walks to the park,
the heat dissolves the avenues.

The Nomenclature cuts across the Arctic:
snare the oil, gas lines, install the stations,
derricks and surveillance towers, surveys, documents,
classified pouches.

Carry this microscopic fissure
into South Asia. Diplomats—they say,
so many teams of men, they orbit in silence and

loud vests and helmets, they stoop with a sweetness
and sift the granules, then, they rise,

oblong, hunched, on fire,
ready to dig into the ice, a new boundary for the national vortex,
this undeclared war; the almost-uttered war, this war begins,
listen. Listen closely—

I hear a rap song in the distance:
"I am standin' in Lebanon
watchin' everbody get it on,
why am I the only one
singin' this desolation song . . . ?"

Enter the Void

I enter the void,
it has the shape of a viola:

Israel, Jenin, West Bank, Nablus—a rubble boy
shifts his scapula as if it was his continent, underground
Gazaground, I want to say—his only bone,

the rubble boy is a girl, I think,
her hair tossed, knotted and torn under
the green shank of fibers, tubes and shells.

She digs for her rubble father, I say rubble
because it is indistinguishable from ice, fire, dust,
clay, flesh, tears, concrete, bread, lungs, pubis, god,
say rubble, say water—

the rubble girl digs for her rubble mother,
occupation—disinheritance—once again,
I had written this somewhere, in a workshop, I think,
yes, it was an afternoon of dark poets with leaves, coffee
and music in the liquor light room.

A rock, perhaps it's a rock, juts out, two rocks
embrace each other, the shapes come to me easily,
an old poetic reflex—memoria, a nation underground,
that is it, the nation under-ground,
that is why the rocks cover it.

I forget to mention the blasts, so many things flying,
light, existence, the house in tins, a mother in rags.

It is too cold to expose her tiny legs,
the fish-shaped back—you must take these notes for me.

Before you go. See this
undulate
extend
beyond
the pools of blood.

I ride the night, past the Yukon, past
South Laredo, past Odessa, past the Ukraine,
old Jaffa, Haifa and Istanbul, across clouds,
hesitant and porous, listen—

they are porous so we can glide
into them, this underbelly, this underground:
wound-mothers and sobbing fathers, they

leave, in their ribboned flesh, shores lisp
against nothingness, open—toward you,
they dissolve again into my shoes—

Hear the dust gong:
gendarme passports,

cloned maize men in C-130's, with tears
bubbling on their hands, pebbles
en route—we are all en route
to the rubblelands.

I want to chant a bliss mantra—
Prajnaparamita
can you hear me?

I want to call for the dragon-slayer omchild.
I am on my knees again.

On the West Bank count
the waves of skull debris—a Hebrew letter
for "love" refuses me,
an Arabic letter for "boundary"
acknowledges me.

Sit on an embankment,
a dust fleece, there is a tidal wave ahead of me.

It will never reach me. I live underground, under the Dead Sea,
under the benevolent rocks and forearms and
mortar shells and slender naked red green
torsos, black,
so much black.
En route:

this could be a train, listen:
it derails into a cloud.

The Women Tell Their Stories

The women tell their stories in Austin,
they tower over the table, their hot work hands
greet me, they speak of their children. The earth
I think, oh, yes, the earth.

Cloned maize men unload another ship through
genetically altered skies and an MC-130 Combat Talon plane
drops into Kandahar, Afghanistan—15,000-pound fuel
air explosives, what is left now? A flower of ethylene and
propylene, then a cluster bomb, filled
with 202 "bomblets"—what am I saying:

Better to say peanut butter, Pop Tarts,
rice and potatoes instead, the same color of village fires,
a yellow can comes down in the name of the Nomenclature.

The question of Kabul, Kashmir, Fallujah
comes up, the question of colonization and
saliva, bacteria in the atoms of expansion drills
into the howling child, this rubble boy:

eat, step lightly on the mines
of the Russian-American war, dear little one
with your folded arms caressing a fender
for shelter.

A Chagall Appears

A Chagall appears, "Nude Over Vitebsk"—
think of her above the mortars, the missiles, think
of her, a perfect sigh above a forlorn homeland, abandoned
many years ago, can you see the floating
unknowable figure?

Then a Dalí, a Warhol, a Varo,
a floating pink-black fish inhales its own slime—
then Siqueiros and his terror fingers scratch
the canvas, this language, they

cannot find this perception. A paramilitary chrysanthemum
opens its filters and appeals to everything in the void.
Listen again:

There are no images
there are no words
there are no sounds
for what is taking place—it has been said
it has been charted. It has been sung,
in the ruins.

Just a boy and his mother
wrapped in bluish muslin sheets from Hebron, Beirut,
then Tel Aviv,
soaked flags dying of thirst, asking for bread,
wine-colors blossom from their bosom; see them,
held up in a gurney, the crowd jeering,
see them?

This shadow is continuous.
This fire is continuous.
This suffering is continuous.

This explosive—well, the laughter from the balcony,
I mean, the spigot
inserted into the mezzo-pump transformer,
that is, the surveillance nose (or shall I say "Security"?)
accelerates toward you,

how shall I say, Nomenclature?
The Thing-Against-Itself
in full regalia. How?

I hold this small tray table that rumbles
in the machine sky
that I am speaking of—

en route: to a city of women
learning to write, read. My own mother, Lucia,
comes to me now—I want to retreat.

A Percentage Will Survive

A percentage will survive—a nuclear scientist
for the Nomenclature speaks now.
A percentage has been scheduled to re-appear,

this sounds something like reincarnation,
something I want to believe.

Nothing of the mother under curfew
en route to a hospital in Bethlehem.
Nothing but cloned maize men.
Nothing but an exotic agent dropped into the cytoplasm,
a new toxin in the clouds has been reserved.
All this lacks definition (on purpose),

it is my nature to lack proportion,
volume, figure, intelligible historicity, time
and its spatial quadrants, remember—rubble,
that is all I truly have—and you.

Pakistan (still dividing)
India (still waiting)
Israel (still subtracting)
Palestine (still subtracting)
Lebanon (still subtracting)
Afghanistan (still waiting)
India again,
Palestine again,
Israel again,

NYC (still falling)—if only I could write
without plots intervening, assassinations, CIA fabulations,
FBI interceptions, Corporate miscalculations,
these silly rhymes are beneath me, they were, yes,
they were—

I haven't told you
about the occupations of the Nomenclature,
I mean inside the Nomenclature's offices, that is,
the treaties on fire, the documents in siege, the Defense Ministers
in the offices setting the plutonium clock hand
a little more to the right, toward you—I haven't spoken

a word about the counterfeit body
in the penthouse growing

at the speed of light, what I mean is—the sun
that is not the sun, it is the hydrogen blast, our spleen
offspring, this curly eyeless child with

an unwritten field in the center of the forehead,
unavailable, classified, a hollow
awaiting fusion—you, and the commedia, the infernos,
or shall I say the Cabinet, the Advisors, the Board,
satellite screws ajar, corporate investment bankers
with their hand down my groin, the accountants
with Picasso Avignon faces, I mean
the re-writer apologists, the agribusiness
pump pesticidal wave, the plague powders en route to you,
forgive me,

if only I could write without the Nomenclature
in between my teeth, the ideology lapel stuck
to my chromosome lines

of afro-indian-hebrew-mestizo-arab-muslim-moorish dancers.
Forgive me.

A Few X's Raise Their Tendrils

A few X's raise their tendrils—
the equations are neutral:
a few Y's lower their ant-shaped abdomens

plusses and minuses, dots, hyphens, additions, accumulations, sausages,
breaded chicken, pheasant and pork, glands in raspberry, infected snouts,
gel from livers, eye-orbits, pancreas and throats, uterus in half, wine
Chablis, Merlot, Chardonnay, St. Michelle Vineyards are best, they say,
in Vallejo, near Napa, try Mondavi, vein fat, cheek meats, turkey head in
parsley sauce, testicles in garlic, more additions, more plates please, every
new nuclear reactor at the table, take a seat, a shower, a plutonium chamber
disguised as an alfalfa truck, West Liberty, Iowa, en route to Yucca
Mountain, a pocked shoulder, neck elongated, pelvis on mustard, salmon
from Bellingham, roast duck in oyster sauce ovary, now

a toast, there is a meadow ahead, a Renoir, is it Fauvist?

Let Me Tell You About My Father, She Says

Let me tell you about my father, she says.
A dark-skinned peasant, a believer in the sacred
aspects of the Mediterranean Sea, at times
he would bow in front of the waves and tell me—
"This, my son, is my audience now, this is who I sing to
every night. One day, you must sing this way too,
do not sing for anything else, my son."

Then, his tattered blue coat, disheveled hat,
stale bread in his pocket. All gone now.

I should tell you more:
My father's kindness, his bravery (the bravery of a peasant).
Once he told me that when he had been stopped
at a check-point, the guard asked him:

"When did you get out?
I thought you were still in prison.
I was the one who arrested you, remember?"

And my father answered—"I got out
the day you went in."

Winds come to me.
Dust, chalk, filaments, threads—needles
that my mother used to mend my pants—
bequeathed to me.

She left me her tiny purse, a pair of glasses
a tiny address book with her favorite sayings
and a journal from the first years after my birth.

"Today, I purchased a bag of oranges.
My little boy seems to like them."

The energy of the young olive trees
behind the fractures and burning figures
wakes me, again, gives me strength.

Lift my head—the pain in my left knee
vanishes. Numbness, sky, a white-yellow covers me.
Smooth my hand across my forehead.

The rubble under my feet is warm,
oxidized, bloody, aromatic, soft, worn, alive.

I sit and write with a pebble.
My sentence: speak little pebble, speak now,
it is your turn.
My sentence coils into itself and stains
my fingers.

If I could write on every shard,
I think they would turn into birds.
I would give them all a new color,
a meadow path, open and clear, with leaves fluttering
and a banquet of old men and aged women
sitting in a circle without the rags, nude,
chamomile and slender blades as new veins,

they would clean stones together,
after a while they

would realize that each stone had the face
of their daughters, the dead ones gone long ago,

the crows on their shoulders
would take to the grasses, flutter—for a moment,

we would look across to Jerusalem, Lebanon,
skip and cross and no one would notice
the land's despair, only the winds, the flaming sunlight as it is—
flame and light.

I have not mentioned the bullets:
they are my universal bliss sound now.

Fool myself again—my musician friends
will understand, my poet friends, well, they know.
So, I run and hide, run and laugh, then hide again,
scoop two handfuls of rubble-ash as if it were
water and so many rivers, wash my face.

I form little ships
with the ash and shards:

follow the nuclear weapons on the submarines,
3,456—count them all for the Nomenclature, they would like this.
Fall back and follow the intercontinental planes
ready to deliver their store of 1,750, don't mention this—
2,000 intercontinental land-based hydrogen bombs,
the Nomenclature wants you to believe in peace, say it,
say it before the volume rises, 2,500 on hair-trigger alert,
I read this somewhere recently,
forget the date, the sources.

I haven't mentioned the Russian numbers.
I haven't mentioned Israel, Pakistan, France, UK, China, India—
(their nuclear numbers).

The birds instead, listen to them, in between the blasts.
How can they still exist? They give me hope, a twisted,
bitter, almost boyish hope. Where do they rest?

They observe you, lift their wings slowly and scroll
through the ground, it is empty, brittle with trails of saliva,
yet they play at being hungry and distracted,
read, examine

a lost city, trilobites, the past, a few seconds
of breath and fresh bread, then they make a new sketch
with long, crooked beaks, a silly scratching sound

X's & Y's & K's
A's & J's & T's

No more than three or five letters at a time.
The birds etch in pairs, in the vast liquid fields,
this borderless rumble of stone-crushers, military orders,
land, the Land you speak of.

Listen,
behind every wall, a tank-eye, a polaroid scanner,
a pod of ire, stoic engines, this uncanny heat blisters

up and down from the void—this new life without
form, this rubble fate.

This Is My Last Report

This is my last report:
I wanted to speak of existence, the ants most of all,
dressed up in their naughty flame-trousers, the exact jaws,
their unknowable kindnesses, their abyss of hungers,
and science, their mercilessness, their prophetic military
devotions, their geometry of scent, their cocoons
for the Nomenclature,

I wanted to speak of the Glue Sniffers
and Glue Smoothers who despise all forms
unbound, loose in their amber nectars, I wanted
to point to their noses, hoses and cables and networks,
their tools, if I can use that word now—and scales and
scanners and Glue Rectories.

I wanted you to meet my broom mother
who carved a hole into her womb
so that I could live—

At every sunset she stands
under the shadow of the watchtowers
elongating and denying her breath.

I wanted to look under the rubble fields
for once, for you (if you approved), flee
into the bullet-riddled openness and fall flat,
arched, askew, under the rubble sheets
and let the rubble fill me

with its sharp plates and ripped dust—
alphabets incomplete and humid. You,
listen,

a little closer
to the chalk dust—this child swinging her left arm,
a ribbon, agitated by unnamed forces, devoured.

WATER

I should have begun with this: the sky
    —WISŁAWA SZYMBORSKA, *from "Sky"*

Descending Tai Shan Mountain

My brother, he is more than that—
to the left, the face of an old man, even though
he is twelve, and I follow him, we pass the shrines and rise through
the green web, a bamboo carved with our names and an oil drum
that hangs in the middle of our arc, this is what we carry, step,
by step, breath by breath, a towel, please,
for my brother, he holds onto the cord between us, four others
behind, stare down, count, you can hear them, on occasion,
whimpering, damning, kick tiny stones from the mortar, my brother
takes his last steps, without seeing, his heart falling,
his knees going up,
this is what we do, every hour, there is no return, only
the uncertain mountain, the mountain.

19 Pokrovskaya Street

My father lights the kerosene lamp, his beard bitten, hands
wet from the river, where he kneels to pray in the mornings,
he sits and pulls out his razor, rummages through a gunnysack,
papers, photos of his children in another country, he cries a little
when he mentions his mother, Benita, and his father, Salomé,
who ran a stable in El Mulato, Chihuahua, eyes cast down
then he points to the mural on the wall, the red
angels descending to earth, naked mothers with bellies giving birth,
lovers in wrinkled green trousers, and a horse with the figures
of children laughing on its back, a goat floats across the night,
a flank of tawdry farmers unfurl into a sparkling forest moon
where elegant birds sit on snowy branches, here is
a miniature virgin where the yellow flames light up the village
one dancer carries fishing poles and easels with diamonds
and other jewels as colors, my father is silent
when he sees these things cut across my face.

Let Me Tell You What a Poem Brings

for Charles Fishman

Before you go further,
let me tell you what a poem brings,
first, you must know the secret, there is no poem
to speak of, it is a way to attain a life without boundaries,
yes, it is that easy, a poem, imagine me telling you this,
instead of going day by day against the razors, well,
the judgments, all the tick-tock bronze, a leather jacket
sizing you up, the fashion mall, for example, from
the outside you think you are being entertained,
when you enter, things change, you get caught by surprise,
your mouth goes sour, you get thirsty, your legs grow cold
standing still in the middle of a storm, a poem, of course,
is always open for business too, except, as you can see,
it isn't exactly business that pulls your spirit into
the alarming waters, there you can bathe, you can play,
you can even join in on the gossip—the mist, that is,
the mist becomes central to your existence.

jjj

ACKNOWLEDGMENTS

I wish to thank Patti Hartmann and Chris Szuter for their unwavering support at the University of Arizona Press during the last decade. Also, many appreciations to all my editors and comrades of the word during the last thirty-eight years: Alurista, Roberto Sifuentes, Walter Lowenfels, Francisco Jimenez, Lauro Flores, Alejandro Murguía, Ishmael Reed, Arthur Vogelsang, Luis Leal, Elaine Katzenberger, Ernesto Padilla, John Marron, Francisco X. Alarcón, Sandy Taylor, Ray Gonzalez, Nicolas Kanellos, Guillermo Gomez-Peña, Alfred Arteaga, David Hamilton, Connie Hales, Dorianne Laux, Kim Addonizio, Andrea Otañez, Ammiel Alcalay, Janet Francendese, Joanna Cotler, Alyson Day, Liz Szabla, Jen Rees, Joyce Jenkins, Francisco Lomelí, Rigoberto Gonzalez, Victor Hernández-Cruz, TR Hummer, Martin Espada, María Herrera-Sobek, Tino Villanueva, Manuel Martin-Rodriguez, Wolfgang Binder, Leroy Quintana, Dana Gioa, Christopher Buckley, Sesshu Foster, Patricia Wakida, Jennifer Joseph, Julie Sopetrán, Julie Kline, Tim Z. Hernandez, Tom Lutz, Ilan Stavans, and many others; without your vision, I would still be standing on the street corner with a bag of poems in my hand. Artists who have lent their eye, heart, and art for my books, gracias— Gloriamalia Flores-Pérez, Rupert García, Yolanda M. López, Cecilia Brunazzi, Patssi Valdez, Alma Lopez, Mario Garza, and Artemio Rodriguez.

Thanks to Stephen Kessler, Sesshu Foster, Dolores Bravo, and Magaly Fernandez, who translated the Spanish poems that appear in *Akrílica*. Due to page limits, I chose only four poems from this book, accompanied by their originals in Spanish.

Many appreciations to all the small presses, magazines, and journals that took my work through the years, in the USA, Mexico, and Latin America—a partial list: *Mid-America Review, La Gente, Antología y Memorias: Memoria del encuentro de literatura de las fronteras, Maize, American Poetry Review, Best American Poetry Review 1992, New England Review, Argonaut, Calafia, University of Arizona Calendar, Lusitania, Poetry Like Bread: Poets of the Political Imagination, Currents from the Dancing River, Antología Histórica y Literaria, Mester, La Voz Urgente: Antología de literatura chicana en español, The Massachusetts Review, The Iowa Review, Under the Pomegranate Tree: The Best New Latino Erotica, Compost, El Coro, Touching the Fire: Fifteen Poets of Today's Latino Renaissance, Luna, Real Things: An Anthology of Popular Culture in American Poetry, Fourteen Hills Review, How Much Earth: An Anthology of Fresno Poets, POG2 Journal, California Poetry: From the Gold Rush to the Present, Lengua Fresca: Latinos Writing on the Edge, BOMB, From the Belly of the Shark: A New Anthology of Native Americans, Festival Flor y Canto: An Anthology of Chicano Literature, Revista Chicano Riqueña, Centzontle: Chicano Short Stories and Poetry, Metamorfosis, Hispamérica, A Través de la Frontera, Palabra Nueva: Poesía Chicana, Contemporary Chicano Poetry: An Anthology, Forward, An Ear to the Ground: An Anthology of Contemporary American Poetry, After Aztlán: Latino Poets of the Nineties, New Visions of Aztlán, The Américas Review, The Boston Review, Alcatraz, The Denver Quarterly, El Tecolote Literario, Obligatory Hug, Oboe6, Red Trapeze, Vórtice, Bombay Gin, The Broken Line/Línea Quebrada, La Neta/Bottom Line, The Soledad Star, Five Fingers Review, As de Corazones Rotos, Espacio Libre, El Excélsior.*

Appreciations to Theatre Degree Zero, from Bisbee, Arizona, for producing *Nuclear Green Night*. And thanks to Gregory Nava and Barbara Martinez-Jitner for taking work for their PBS *American Family* productions.

For permission to reprint various poems, thank you: Lalo Press, Arte Público Press, Dragon Cloud Press, City Lights Publishers, Curbstone Press, Manic D Press, and Stephen Kessler from Alcatraz Editions.

For a great teacher, Marvin Bell.

A lotus garden for my children—Robert, Almasol, Joshua, Marlene, and Joaquín Ramón—for their patience and love. And grandchildren—Rainsong, Jeremiah, Arissa, Ethan, Bella, Dylan Raoul, Luna Sohalia, and Cyrus.

Deep bows for my mother, Lucha Quintana, who cast me as a poet, and my father, Felipe Emilio Herrera, who unraveled the road.

Om Mani Padme Hum

ABOUT THE AUTHOR

After serving as chair of the Chicano and Latin American Studies Department at California State University–Fresno, in 2005 Juan Felipe Herrera joined the Creative Writing Department at the University of California–Riverside, as Tomás Rivera Endowed Chair and director of the Art and Barbara Culver Center for the Arts, a new multimedia space in downtown Riverside. In 1990 he was a teaching fellow with the Distinction of Excellence at the University of Iowa Writers' Workshop. Also, he has taught at the New College of San Francisco and Stanford University.

During the last three decades, Juan Felipe has received numerous awards and fellowships, such as two National Endowment for the Arts Writers' Fellowships, four California Arts Council grants, the UC Berkeley Regents' Fellowship, the Breadloaf Fellowship in Poetry, and the Stanford Chicano Fellows Fellowship. He has given lectures, workshops, readings, and performances of his work and writing throughout the nation.

Juan Felipe's publications in the last decade include fourteen collections of poetry, prose, writing and plays, short stories, young adult novels, and picture books for children, with twenty-one books in total. For his literary endeavors, Juan Felipe has garnered the Ezra Jack Keats Award, the Hungry Mind Award of Distinction, the Americas Award, the Focal Award, the Pura Belpré Honors Award, the Smithsonian Children's Book of the Year, the Cooperative Children's Book Center Choice, the IRA Teacher's Choice, the Los Angeles Times Book Award nomination, the Texas Blue Bonnet nomination, the New York Public Library outstanding book for high school students, the National Tomás Rivera Mexican American Award, and two Latino Hall of Fame Poetry awards.

Juan Felipe is also an actor, with appearances on film and stage. He recently produced "The Twin Tower Songs," a San Joaquin Valley performance memorial on the September 11th tragedy, and he writes poetry sequences for the PBS television series *American Family*. His 2004 musical, *The Upside Down Boy*, was well received in New York City (attended by 9,000 K–6 students). It was produced by Making Books Sing, with libretto by Barbara Zinn Krieger, lyrics by Juan Felipe Herrera, and music by Cristian Amigo. More recently, he wrote the libretto and lyrics for *Salsalandia*, a commission for the La Jolla Playhouse.

Juan Felipe is a board member of the Before Columbus American Book Awards Foundation. He received his B.A. in social anthropology from the University of California at Los Angeles, his M.A. in social anthropology from Stanford, and his M.F.A. in creative writing from the Writers' Workshop at the University of Iowa. Juan Felipe often travels and performs with his partner, Margarita Robles, a poet and performance artist.

CONTENTS OF AUDIO CD

This book includes an audio CD of selected poems and conversations in twenty-four tracks recorded on June 13, 2007.

Producer: Tim Labor, University of California, Riverside

Special thanks to Paul Richardson, Walter Clark, University of California, Riverside, Riverside Department of Music.

TRACK		COLLECTION	DURATION
1.	A Certain Man	*A Certain Man*	1:09
2.	[Let Us Gather in a Flourishing Way]	*Rebozos of Love*	2:04
3.	Exiles	*Exiles of Desire*	4:00
4.	Inside the Jacket	*Facegames*	1:35
5.	Foreign Inhabitant	*Facegames*	2:31
6.	She Wants the Ring Like He Wants the Suit of Scars / But	*Akrílica*	1:37
7.	Ella quiere el anillo como aquél quiere el traje de la cicatriz / Pero	*Akrílica*	1:30
8.	Iowa Blues Bar Spiritual	*Night Train to Tuxtla*	5:40
9.	IV. Jade Mother Goddess	*The Roots of a Thousand Embraces*	2:08
10.	7:30 pm / Thursday	*Love After the Riots*	1:45
11.	3:07 am	*Love After the Riots*	1:21
12.	Angel Wrestler (with blonde wig)	*Border-Crosser with a Lamborghini Dream*	3:07

TRACK		COLLECTION	DURATION
13.	La Lotería	*Lotería Cards and Fortune Poems*	2:01
14.	La Rosa	*Lotería Cards and Fortune Poems*	1:24
15.	Pascuala III	*Thunderweavers*	2:45
16.	Pascuala III	*Tejedoras de rayos*	0:41
17.	Pascuala XI	*Thunderweavers*	0:41
18.	Pascuala XI	*Tejedoras de rayos*	0:44
19.	Giraffe on Fire #26	*Giraffe on Fire*	3:05
20.	Óyeme Mamita: Standing on 20th and Harrison	*Notebooks of a Chile Verde Smuggler*	2:43
21.	This Is My Last Report	*The Five Elements*	2:15
22.	Enter the Void	*The Five Elements*	3:58
23.	19 Pokrovskaya Street	*The Five Elements*	1:46
24.	Let Me Tell You What a Poem Brings	*The Five Elements*	1:49
25.	Dedications	*Live at the recording studio*	0:37